Living LANGUAGE

EDITORIAL WRITING

John Shuttleworth

Hodder & Stoughton

A MEMBER OF THE HODDER HEADLINE GROUP

Acknowledgements

The publishers would like to thank the following for their kind permission to reproduce copyright material:

Texts 2, 3, 4, 5, 7 and 8 reproduced by kind permission of the Northern Examinations and Assessment Board; text 12 © The Stationery Office; text 13 reproduced from *J–17* 30 October 1996; text 15 from *Wildlife of Britain* Issue 4 © Midsummer Books Ltd; text 17 reproduced by kind permission of Edexcel; text 19 reproduced by kind permission of NSPCC; text 20 from *The Face of Battle* by John Keegan © Jonathan Cape Ltd; text 23 from *Intimate Voices* © Galloping Dog Press; text 25 *The 'Azards o' Chimuck Szwippin'* by K. Morgan; text 25 *Talkin' Brooad* by Kenneth Wadsworth © The Littlewood Press; text 26 *The Queen's English* from 'Selected Poems' by Tony Harrison © Penguin Books; text 30 *Kidspoem/Bairnsang* by Liz Lochhead from 'Dreaming Frankenstein and Collected Poems' © Polygon; text 53 from *The Incredible Music Machine* by J. Lowe, R. Miller and R. Boan © Quartet Books.

Every effort has been made to trace copyright holders of material reproduced in this book. Any rights not acknowledged will be acknowledged in subsequent printings if notice is given to the publisher.

Orders: please contact Bookpoint Ltd, 130 Milton Park, Abingdon, Oxon OX14 4SB. Telephone: (44) 01235 827720 , Fax: (44) 01235 400454. Lines are open from 9.00–6.00, Monday to Saturday, with a 24 hour message answering service. You can also order through our website at www.hodderheadline.co.uk

British Library Cataloguing in Publication Data
A catalogue record for this title is availabe from The British Library

ISBN 0 340 73084 6

First published 1999
Impression number   10 9 8 7 6 5
Year   2005 2004 2003

Cover photo from Ronald Grant Archive.
Typeset by Fakenham Photosetting Limited, Fakenham, Norfolk.
Printed in Great Britain for Hodder & Stoughton Educational, a division of Hodder Headline, 338 Euston Road, London NW1 3BH by J. W. Arrowsmith Ltd, Bristol.

CONTENTS

1   Getting Started   1

2   Be Conventional   16

3   Are You Well Structured?   33

4   Get Weaving   46

5   Finding the Right Voice   58

6   Do-it-Yourself   71

7   It's the Real Thing   78

1 Getting Started

In this chapter you will learn how to prepare to answer those English Language examination tasks in which you have to construct a new text from a selection of texts provided for you as source material. This task is known as the Case Study, the Desk Study or Textual Recasting, depending on the syllabus you are following. You will learn the importance of careful, *purposeful* reading and will thus be prepared to cope with anything the examiners may give you.

TEXT 1

HAMPSHIRE NEWS AGENCY: 93 Just's Road, Portsmouth PO8 6DT 01706 675430

TOWING – Date/Time Sent: Monday 26 January 1998 10:07:12 am

A man was rescued from freezing seas after he was spotted trying to SWIM ashore TOWING his young son behind him in the middle of winter:

An amazed coastguard who spotted 30 year old Ted Curtis hauling the dinghy through the waves alerted the rescue services.

Ted plunged overboard into the sea while trying to restart the engine of his dinghy off Gosport in Hampshire.

While his seven year old son Jonathan sat in the boat, Ted grabbed a trailing line and struck out for shore.

A Portsmouth Coastguard spokesman said: 'I don't know whether he couldn't get back into the boat or whether he thought he might capsize it trying.

But when he was spotted by an auxiliary coastguard, he was trying to swim ashore towing the boat with his son in it.

The dinghy was about 100 yards from the shore. He wasn't making very good headway, and of course the water was exceptionally cold. He was lucky someone spotted him.'

An RAF helicopter team was sent to the scene and they lifted Ted to safety from the water and took him to hospital.

Then they went back to pick up Jonathan who had waited in the dinghy for his rescuers.

Ted, from Cosham and Jonathan are now safely back at home recovering from their ordeal after treatment for hypothermia.

You have just read one of the hundreds of stories that every day pour into national newspaper offices. News agencies, like the one which produced this story send such items from their local area to all national papers in the hope that they will be published and thus make some money for the agency. Of course, of the very few that actually make it into the national press, hardly any will appear in exactly the same words as the agency's original story. Sub-editors may re-structure it, highlight particular aspects or re-write it in the style of the newspaper for which they are working. If it appears at all, the story will be written in a different style in, say, the *News of the World* than in the *Independent*. They will also write a suitable headline and ensure that the story is the exact length to fit the space available. This may involve abbreviating or sometimes even expanding the story.

ACTIVITY 1

Imagine that you are the sub-editor working on the home news pages of a national newspaper. You have just received this story from the Hampshire News Agency and you decide to include it in tomorrow's paper. Re-write the story as it would appear in your paper. You will therefore need to:

- choose a paper to work for;
- ensure that you are familiar with its style and treatment of such stories;
- decide on the 'angle' you wish to take on the story so that it will appeal to your readers;
- write the story;
- write a headline;
- decide how many words you will allocate to it.

If you are working as part of a group, you should each choose a different newspaper so that you can compare your results.

COMMENTARY

The activity that you have just been working on is obviously one that not only has 'real-life' practical applications, especially for aspiring journalists but is also one that has great similarities to the work that you undertake as part of your A-Level English Language course. You have had to:

- read a text paying close attention both to its content and style;
- re-present it for a specific audience (the readers of your chosen newspaper) and for a specific purpose (to inform and, possibly, entertain your readers);
- select, structure and re-organise the original material;
- write your new text for a very specific genre (newspapers) and in a particular style (that of your chosen paper).

In fact, the only difference between the re-writing and re-presenting of this story from what you have to do at A-Level is that here you were free to choose the number of words in the new text for yourself.

You might be surprised at how short the treatment of this story was in one national newspaper. Here it is, without its accompanying picture:

Frozen Ted Curtis, 30, had to be rescued from the sea off Gosport, Hampshire, yesterday after he plunged into icy waters to tow his son Jonathan, seven, and their conked-out dinghy ashore.

Being able to produce effective newspaper stories is not the only type of writing that you will have the chance to practise and perfect during this part of your English Language course. Publicity handouts, radio scripts, advertisements, educational packs, advice leaflets and magazine articles are just some of the types (or genres and sub-genres) of writing that you are likely to be working on. You can see that in this way you'll be equipped to become a much better and more professional writer. Not only will you become a much more skilful *writer*, you'll also become a much more skilful *reader*, because in preparing to produce your new texts, you'll have to read a number of source texts very carefully and purposefully. Such skills, of course, are useful not only in helping you succeed in examinations, but could also be very necessary during your working life.

For example, you could be working for a large charity, such as the NSPCC, and you could be asked to produce the text for a leaflet that was to form part of a mail shot to raise money from prospective donors. The leaflet was to be a hard-hitting and emotional appeal, yet must be factually based. You were provided with a comprehensive set of official documents, reports and statistics on which to base your text. You would, of course, have to adapt your sources for the particular audience and purpose of the mail shot and would thus be employing exactly the same skills as you did in your English Language course.

Or, take a second illustration. You might be asked to write a short information and instruction leaflet to be included in a tube of pain-killing ointment. The leaflet, you are told, is to explain clearly and unambiguously to the patient what the ointment can do, when and how it should be applied and, perhaps most importantly of all, what the patient must *not* do with it. The manufacturer has given you a number of documents about the ointment, but these are obviously too technical for the patients to understand, as they were originally produced for medical scientists. It becomes your job to adapt them for their new purpose and audience.

We have seen that some of the work you will be undertaking during your A-Level course and consequently the skills that you acquire will equip you to produce more effective, practical pieces of writing, such as the one with which we began this chapter. However, to take any A-Level subject means that you will have to face, sooner or later, writing of a very specific kind – in other words, examination papers. What, then, can you expect to be asked to do at the end of this part of your English Language course?

Though there may well be different names for the paper you will be taking, which depend on the particular examination board's syllabus you are following, what you have to do differs little from syllabus to syllabus. You will:

- be provided with a number of written extracts of differing lengths from a variety of sources. The extracts will be on the same subject, but may well deal with different aspects of it or take different perspectives on it;
- have to read the extracts through very carefully at least once. Some examination boards allow you time to do this reading before sitting the paper – others provide you with the material only in the examination itself;
- have to prepare the material thoroughly to enable you to tackle the assignment the examiner has set. This may entail summarising, linking and re-structuring the material, for example;

■ have to produce, in response to a task set by examiners, a piece of writing that re-presents the source material. Typically, this will involve you writing for a different audience, for a different purpose and in a different genre and format than any you encountered in the sources.

Two illustrations should help to make this clearer:

1 Based on a file of material about the events in Beijing's Tiananmen Square in June 1989, you could be asked to produce a short radio script for GCSE pupils who were studying contemporary world history. A similar assignment was set by one exam board in 1998.
2 Based on a file of material about the history of tin mining and the abandoned mines, you could be asked to produce a report for Cornwall County Council on the tourist and heritage potential of the now defunct industry.

Assessment Objectives

You can see that in writing such assignments, you'll have fulfilled a number of the Assessment Objectives for Advanced Level English Language. Assessment Objectives are what all A-Level syllabuses test and there are ones for English Language, ones for Geography, ones for Biology and so on. Therefore you should make sure you know exactly what the objectives are for each subject you take, because examiners will be looking to see if, in your answers, you have demonstrated your mastery of them. The main one you will be fulfilling in this part of the examination is part of:

AO4 demonstrate expertise and accuracy in writing for a variety of specific purposes and audiences.

but others do come into play.

It is the aim of this book to help you prepare for and tackle successfully this type of question or assignment and to that end you'll be looking at:

■ how to read, select and edit the source material;
■ how to recognise different types of text and their associated conventions;
■ how to weave together your new text and write any necessary new material such as an introduction, links, captions and a conclusion;
■ how to rewrite, paraphrase and summarise where necessary;
■ how to construct your new text so that its structure and sequence are clear to the reader or listener;
■ how to address the reader (or listener) in an appropriate voice.

Having completed these sections successfully, not only should you be able to score very highly in an examination, but you will have been equipped with reading and writing skills that will be valuable in contexts other than an examination hall. In a very real sense then, these are life-skills.

The remainder of this chapter will suggest the ways in which you can read and prepare the source material you will use to create your new text.

Learning to read

'Oh come on! I already know how to read. I've been doing it ever since I was five (or whatever). I don't need to be taught again.' This might very well be your quick response to the title of this section, especially in a book on *Advanced Level* English Language, but what the title is drawing your attention to is the fact that developing and honing your reading skills is of paramount importance if you want to succeed in these writing assignments. Remember, you've been given a lengthy amount of time (up to three days by one exam board) to read the source material, so it's up to you to use this time profitably. They wouldn't have given you this time if reading weren't a very important part of preparation for the exam. *Reading*, of course, is a term that can cover a variety of approaches to texts – there are lots of different ways of reading: just think of some of the expressions we have for it. You can *skim, survey* or *study, peruse, pore over* or *piece together*, for example.

However, it's vital that you read the texts in the source file very carefully. Of course, your first 'reading' of the material may well be a quick skim through to give yourself an overall impression of the texts, but if that is the only type of reading that you do, then you will find the writing of the assignment very difficult indeed. The key to a successful answer is a careful and purposeful reading of the sources. You'll notice that the word 'purposeful' appeared in the previous sentence and it was used because it's important that you read the texts *with* purpose. It's all too easy to read, re-read and re-read the texts and to think that you are preparing effectively for the assignment when, in fact, all that you are doing is to remind yourself of what the texts are about and, in addition, to bore yourself rigid. Yes, you will read the texts a number of times in preparation, but you'll be reading them with a different purpose in mind each time. It's rather like having different pairs of glasses. There are people who have glasses for distance and glasses for reading and they are constantly swapping between the pairs, depending on what they want to see at a particular time. You too will be changing glasses, as it were, when you read the source material because of the different purposes for your reading. Let's turn, then, to your first purpose in reading.

What's the provenance?

You are going to be faced with a number of texts to read on the same subject and the first thing you will need to do is to 'interrogate' each text to establish its provenance. This isn't as difficult as it might sound, but if you do it properly, it will prevent you from making silly mistakes when you come to compose your new text. To establish the provenance of a text means discovering:

- who wrote the text;
- when the text was written;
- who the text was written for; and
- the genre and purpose of the text.

You need to have as much information as possible before you start to write your assignment. Suppose you had been asked to write a tourist guide to the important sites of industrial archaeology in Avon and one of your pieces of source material was taken from a book about Gloucestershire, published in 1936. If you used material from this book, not only would much of it be out of date, but you would be in danger of writing about areas outside Avon, because of the changes in county boundaries. Not all of Gloucestershire found itself in the new county of Avon. Or, to give you another example: suppose you had been asked to write the script for a talk for primary school children on looking after guinea pigs and you'd included in your talk, without adapting it, material from a book on Animal Physiology written by a university lecturer to prepare undergraduate vets for their examinations. You'd be very likely to lose the interest of a very critical audience, who would become increasingly restless!

So you can see that it's important for you to get clear in your mind this information about provenance and, luckily, it's not too difficult for you to discover as both the author (and sometimes her or his qualifications or status) and the date of publication are usually given, along with the original title of the work. So, make sure you use this information! Clearly an extract from a book called *Narcissistic Narrative: The Metafictional Paradox* (1984) by Linda Hutcheon, Professor of English and Comparative Literature at the University of Toronto would need considerable adaptation if your audience were GCSE students. But, of course, so would *Happy Venture Playbook One: Story Time* (1951) by Fred J Schonell!

You need, as well, to establish the purpose of the text you are reading and this isn't always as easy to do. An author may have a number of different purposes in mind when writing. However, it will be easier for you in the initial classification of the texts if you limit purpose to four broad categories:

- to entertain;
- to advise or instruct;
- to inform;
- to persuade.

Some texts you are working with will have one clear purpose: a car maintenance manual is designed to instruct, a book of jokes for children is designed to entertain. With some other texts it may not be so easy: for example, though the primary purpose of advertisements is to persuade, many are very entertaining; though the primary purpose of an Income Tax leaflet may be to inform, it may also contain instructions. So, when looking for a text's purpose, it may be best at this stage to seek to discover its *primary* purpose.

To give you some practice in identifying the provenance and primary purpose of texts, here are four short pieces taken from the source file for a recent examination. They are all on the same subject – feeding guinea pigs. Read each text carefully and for each one:

1 identify –
   a the intended audience;
   b the primary purpose of the text;
   c what the text can tell us about the author;
   d what type or genre of text the extract is taken from.
2 match the text with its source. The four titles from which they were taken follow the texts. Give reasons for your decisions.

TEXT 2

Principles of guinea pig nutrition

The guinea pig, like humans and apes, is unable to synthesise its own vitamin C (ascorbic acid) as it lacks the enzyme L-gulonolactone oxidase which is required to convert L-gulono-lactone to L-ascorbic acid. It therefore requires a daily supply of vitamin C. The normal requirement for vitamin C is 10 mg/kg, and this increases to 20 mg/kg during pregnancy. If vitamin C is added to the drinking water in the form of soluble tablets (T× 54) it must be given via a dish or a bottle with a stainless steel nozzle. Other metals will accelerate the decomposition of ascorbic acid. Rosehip syrup is a useful alternative which can be added to the drinking water to provide extra vitamin C. It should be diluted with water to produce a solution containing 12 mg per 100 ml of vitamin C. The daily requirements for this vitamin will be met as long as a balanced diet of dry food, carrots and greens is fed. The vitamin C content of dried food will deteriorate over 9–12 weeks, so deficiency problems will arise if the dry food is stale. Rabbit food is also unsuitable as it does not contain adequate amounts of this vitamin.

TEXT 3

Feeding your pet

You should be able to keep your pet in perfect condition by making sure that it eats the right sorts of food in the right amounts. Just as with humans, overeating or eating too much of one particular type of food can lead to a fat and lazy pet that is not much fun as a companion.

The correct diet for rabbits and guinea pigs is basically green vegetables and fruit, cabbages, carrots, apples, pears etc. You should complement this with some dried food such as oats or nuts or a packaged food – do not overdo this, as it could lead to a weight problem. Hay should always be available either in the hay rack or as bedding, but ensure that it is clean and changed regularly.

TEXT 4

Vitamin C deficiency

Guinea pigs, and especially pregnant sows, have a particular need for a high daily vitamin C intake. A deficiency may lead to scurvy, and a loss of resistance to other diseases, although no such risk occurs if the diet is high in fresh, raw fruit and vegetable, grass and suitable wild plants. Guinea pigs not feeding adequately because of overgrown teeth (p 6) may not take in enough of the vitamin, even though the right foods are available to them. Pellets fed without fresh vegetable matter, or those prepared for other animals, may not contain enough vitamin C to meet this need.

TEXT 5

Checklist

- hutch
- outdoor run
- wood chips
- hay for bedding
- food dishes
- drip-feed water bottle
- food:
      guinea pig cereal mix
      (**and/or** guinea pig pellets)
      fresh vegetables
      hay (the same as for bedding)
      vitamin drops
      mineral block
- small branch or block of hardwood
- grooming brush
- cleaning utensils and materials
- carrying box

Titles
Care for Your Guinea Pig – The Official RSPCA Handbook
Diseases of Domestic Guinea Pigs V C G Richardson
Looking After Your Guinea Pig H Piers
Pets for Children one of a series of *Talking Pets* leaflets.

This is a suggested answer in note form for Text 2:

Audience: A knowledgeable and specialised one – vets or trainee vets? Much technical vocabulary: *enzyme L-gulanolactone oxidase*, which the writer does not gloss for the audience. Also, formal vocabulary: *accelerate the decomposition*.

Purpose: To inform

Author: An expert on guinea pig nutrition. Possibly a vet or university lecturer?

Genre: A textbook – numbered headings and sub-headings to make it easier for the reader to find his or her way around the text.

ACTIVITY 3

The next activity is a little more challenging. The subject is still diet, but this time, not a guinea pig's but a child's. The passage that follows is one constructed from *three* separate extracts about children's nutrition. The sentences from the three passages have been mixed together. You have to:

- decide which sentences are from each passage;
- re-assemble them in the correct order;
- then, for each passage, decide what
  a is the primary purpose; and
  b the intended audience.

TEXT 6

You can compare a child's body, in one way, to a building under construction.

More anxiety is expressed over their infant's feeding by mothers, in routine contacts with health visitors, than any other topic.

Yet sadly for many adults and children these days it is often fresh food that is the novelty.

The inclusion of highly flavoured, sweet and savoury processed foods and drinks in a child's diet usually blunts the appetite and upsets food choice at mealtimes.

There was an association between the two symptoms:

of the 1727 children with feeding difficulties as a baby, 670 (39%) had also had sleeping problems at that time.

Before we talk about the everyday foods that children can eat, we ought to discuss the more important chemical substances that foods are composed of, and what the body uses them for.

One of the best ways to ensure that your young family eats the best is to keep only 'healthy' food in the house – fruit, vegetables, nuts, seeds, raisins, home-made bread, biscuits and cakes, unsweetened fruit juices – that way the children can eat anything they like!

But a human being is also a machine that's running.

A lot of different materials are needed to build it and keep it in repair.

In retrospect, though, the proportion of mothers reporting feeding problems when the child was a baby was, at 13.3%, very similar to the proportion reporting the child as having had frequent sleeping difficulties as a baby (13.8%).

Most convenience foods are made to high standards of hygiene but few are meant, so the manufacturers say, to be eaten exclusively in place of fresh and wholefoods.

It requires fuel for energy, and other substances to make it work properly, just as a car needs petrol, oil, grease, water.

Is it contradictory?

Don't be surprised if you find that some passages in the sources contradict each other. You should always be on the lookout for them, as examiners often like to include them to test your ability not only to read carefully, but also to see whether you can handle these contradictions in the construction of your own answer, if you have to. There are two main reasons for contradictions. The first is because writers included in the source material sometimes hold opposing views on subjects; the second is often a result of the circumstances under which a passage has been written. Think, for example, of two newspaper reports that carry contradictory information about a terrorist bombing or a motorway pile-up. One of the reports might have been written by a journalist who was an on-the-spot eye-witness phoning through the story as it happened. The pressure of events could well cause some factual errors to appear in the initial report that would be corrected in later editions.

ACTIVITY 4

Look at the following two passages used in a recent examination in which opposing views are put forward. They are both about transporting used nuclear fuel. The first is from a leaflet published by British Nuclear Fuels Ltd and the second is from the Internet website of N-BASE, an organisation concerned about nuclear pollution. Read them carefully. In what ways do N-BASE's views contradict those of BNFL?

TEXT 7

To make sure transporting all types of radioactive materials is safe, the design of all transport containers follows rules at least as strict as those laid down by the International Atomic Energy Agency (IAEA). The IAEA also sets the standards for strict impact and fire tests to check that the containers can withstand the most serious accident and that no radioactivity will escape.

These tests include two 'drop' tests – one onto a solid surface and the other onto a steel spike. These surfaces are made from reinforced concrete and steel and are built so they do not move when hit by the flask. This means that most of the force is directed back into the flask when it hits the surface.

These tests are far more demanding than staged accidents. As an example, in 1984 a demonstration was carried out at a British Rail test track at Leicester. A 140 tonne train, travelling at 100 miles an hour was

driven into a flask which had been placed on the track in its most vulnerable position. Although the train was destroyed the crash made only one-third of the damage that a flask would receive from the series of tests set by the IAEA. It came as no surprise to us that the flask in the train crash received only minor damage.

In the USA, tests have also been carried out to show the safety of nuclear fuel flasks. At Sandia, in New Mexico, a flask on a lorry was driven at 60 miles an hour into a huge concrete block. The flask suffered so little damage that it was cleaned and used again in a similar test, this time at 80 miles an hour. Again, the flask passed this very severe test.

Another test which the IAEA carry out on flasks is to put the flask in a fire of 800 degrees centigrade for 30 minutes. At Sandia, in a special fire test, a flask was placed over burning fuel for 90 minutes, this is three times longer than the time set out in the regulations. Temperatures reached 1400 degrees centigrade on the flask's surface but it did not break and the water inside the flask did not overheat.

TEXT 8

Despite industry assurances about the safety of the flasks used to transport spent fuel and the fact that there has been no major incident involving flasks, the international standards are widely considered too low – the United States has much higher standards for flasks than the current safety standards of the

International Atomic Energy Authority. The US demands flasks withstand an impact speed of 464 km/h compared with 48 km/h for the IAEA.

Under current IAEA standards for withstanding fires a flask must withstand a fire of 800C for 30–60 minutes – the US standard is 760C for an hour. Research has shown, however, that fires on ships often burn at up to 2000C and at least a day. In the UK in 1985 there was an often quoted test conducted to show how tough a flask was when an empty train was crashed into the 368mm thick steel side of a flask used to transport Magnox spent fuel. The industry used this test to illustrate flask safety – but other flasks, often taking spent fuel from Japan to the UK have 90mm sides together with 160mm lead lining. Also the Department of Transport has accepted the test subjected the flask to only about half the present IAEA standard.

Chapter 7 contains further examples of work based on this question about the nuclear industry.

Putting the texts into categories

You are now in a position to move on to the next stage of your reading in preparation for an assignment. Although the texts you will be dealing with are all concerned with the same general subject, your aim should be to group numbers of them together under a series of headings or categories that describe more specifically the content of the material. Don't be too ambitious here; you will find that five or six categories are more than enough to work with. Any more would be pointless as you could find yourself putting each text into a separate category; whilst having only a small number of categories would be equally pointless as you could almost be back to square one with all the texts being under the same heading as in the original source file.

Now that you have made yourself familiar with the material, your first step should be to decide what the categories to which you will assign the texts are to be. Make a list of the categories and then mark each page of the source file and/or extract with the heading of the category that best fits it. In this way, you'll have a quick reference guide to the total content of the material. It's quite possible that some of the extracts may be labelled more than once. Don't worry – this is only to be expected. For example, you may be dealing with a selection of extracts on the French sculptor Rodin and two of the categories you select may be *Rodin's Methods of Working* and the famous sculpture called *The Thinker*. One of the extracts may deal with Rodin's preparatory work for *The Thinker* and would therefore fall into both of your categories. You could find this dual labelling occurring quite often.

Sometimes, you might find that you could sub-divide your categories. You might, for instance, have to work on material about the 1990s war between Bosnia and Serbia (in the former Yugoslavia) and discover a number of pieces amongst the many in the file that could be generally labelled *War's Effects on Sarajevo*. You could perhaps categorise these pieces further by labelling them *War's Effects on Sarajevo – eye witness accounts* and *War's Effects on Sarajevo – social and economic* and so on, but they would still have been placed under the main heading.

This system of multiple labelling will make it much easier for you to have different perspectives on the material and to think about the different approaches you might take when you are asked to weave together your new text. To go into the exam room having a pre-conceived notion of how you are going to treat the texts or even having a pre-conceived (but wrong) idea that you will be asked to write a radio script, or whatever, is a recipe for disaster because it won't allow you to have a flexible response to the task that has been set. The approach as outlined here should prevent this from happening. Even if you are taking an exam in which you know the task as you prepare the material, you should still adopt this approach.

Don't worry if some of the material you have to read doesn't fit neatly into the various categories you have chosen. There may be overlap or you may feel that certain pieces (or sections of pieces) could fit into more than one of your categories. This activity isn't like a jigsaw in which all the pieces lock perfectly together. The process you are undertaking can't be so exact.

You may even find that some of the pieces seem to have little connection with the rest of the material. Remember, this could be a deliberate ploy on the examiner's part, as one of the skills you are being tested on is to see if you can select material that is relevant to a particular task. If all the material you are given *is* relevant, then this particular skill will not really be tested.

By this stage of your preparation, you should:

■ have a clear view of the provenance (author, date, audience, purpose and genre) of each text;

■ have assigned each text to a category.

Making connections

Now that you know the content of the material thoroughly and have assigned it to specific categories, the next stage of your preparation is to begin to make links between the various texts. These will have been presented to you in a totally random order, but you are expected to demonstrate your ability to structure your new text clearly. This is fully covered in Chapter 3, but you can make your writing task much easier if you begin to make connections between the texts during your reading and preparation time. This is, in effect, the third pair of reading glasses you are using.

Of course, there are no hard and fast rules here, as the order or sequence you impose on the material will be yours and yours alone. It will depend both on the content of the texts and on your own personal preferences, but you will have already made a start when you assigned the pieces to different categories.

Here are a few suggestions as to the kind of connections that are possible, but remember they are only suggestions; examiners are always pleased to find candidates who have structured their answers in ways that the examiners themselves had not anticipated.

- If the material was produced at different times, it may be appropriate to sequence it according to the dates of composition.
- If the material refers to historical events, you could sequence it chronologically.
- If the material presents differing facets of an argument or differing points of view, you could choose to group together those on one side of the argument before grouping those on the other; or you might choose to present one piece from one side and then one from the other and so on.
- You could sequence the material according to the contrasting tones of voice adopted by the writers.
- It might be appropriate to group together all the pieces that were written for a particular audience. For example, pieces that were written for experts in a subject could contrast with those written for beginners.

These are only suggestions and you will very probably come up with better ideas, as different topics will suggest different approaches, but the important thing to remember is that to impose an order or structure on a variety of texts is better than no order whatsoever. Chaos won't get you very far.

Summarise the material

By this stage, you will be very familiar indeed with the content of the extracts, but it can sometimes be extremely useful both as a way to fix them even more securely in your mind and as an aide-memoire in the exam to summarise each substantial piece in no more than two or three short sentences. Of course, some pieces are easier to summarise than others. Factual and informative pieces lend themselves to summary better than do pieces in which the writer is trying to persuade you to adopt a particular set of beliefs or attitudes, for instance. Nor is it worth summarising any very short pieces which you may be given.

Annotate the material

The final stage involves annotating the texts in more detail. If you do this, it will be easier for you to find what you want during the exam. Then, you won't have the time to go through all the texts to find exactly what you want. Facts and figures have an annoying habit of hiding themselves just when you need to refer to them! So you should develop your own system of annotation to avoid such problems when under examination stress.

Obviously, you'll need most of the time in the exam to reflect on, plan and actually write your own text. Here are a few suggestions for annotation that seem to work well.

- Make cross-references. This will help you to identify those pieces of information (or ideas, opinions and theories) which should be considered together. You should devise a system of margin notes. For example: 'see page 13 lines 35–58'.
- Underline or highlight key phrases, names or dates, though you should do this sparingly. If you underline too much in a text, then the exercise becomes self-defeating as the purpose is to highlight only the most important material. A passage that has almost everything underlined tells you almost nothing. Avoid your texts becoming a kaleidoscope of colour.
- You could use colour coding to give a quick visual marker or indication of the contents of each page. As an example, imagine you have been given a set of texts about a famous pianist who had moved into conducting. You might devise a colour code like this:
  blue: early life
  red: career as a pianist
  green: career as a conductor
  pink: adult and private life.

Again the same warning applies: use the colour sparingly. Overuse of colour will confuse rather than clarify.

These, then, are the activities you should undertake in your preparation. Obviously, there isn't the space in this short book to print out a full set of extracts for you to practise your preparatory work, but your teachers will be able to provide you with some, or you could always put together some of your own for your group to work on.

However, it will be useful to close this chapter with an example of what one student did as she prepared for her Case Study exam. The set of extracts that she was working on was about Pressure Groups and consisted of material on Amnesty International, Greenpeace, CND and other smaller pressure groups together with information written for magistrates about the law on meetings and demonstrations. Having followed the advice given in this chapter, she wrote a summary sheet, part of which is reproduced here, that she could refer to in the examination. The fact that she gained a Grade A suggests that her thorough preparation was very worthwhile.

It is worth looking closely at what proved so useful to her. You'll notice that for each text she has:

- identified the provenance;
- summarised very succinctly the content;
- suggested an order in which they might be placed; and
- put them into categories.

She has been extremely thorough and, most importantly, has written her notes so that they are easy to follow in the pressurised situation of the exam – and has made them legible.

Figure 1 (this has been typeset for clarity, but the original was handwritten).

TITLE	*AUTHOR*	*SUMMARY*	*PURPOSE*	*GENRE*	*AUDIENCE*	*TONE*	*DATE*
CND as a P.G.	CND member	Aims of CND, structure, Put pressure on	To inform about organisation in a favourable light - persuade people to join	Fact Sheet + Logo	For students - A level Pol, GCSE Bus Studies etc	Simple, long, formal, favourable	1995
In Brief - The Campaign for Nuclear Disarmament	"	Methods, who joins, summary	As above	"	"	"	"
"	"	What stand for, how campaign, how people can help	Persuade people to join + historical info of past events	CND newsletter + photo	CND members, adults, teens	Dramatic to evoke enthusiasm for CND	90s
"	"	Risk of deterrence, past achievements, how it started, 80s, 90s, safety	"	"	"	"	"
Amnesty Int. Urgent Action	Amnesty members	Peru: Canto Grande prisoners. Background + general info	Inform favourably about events which have happened, to compel action	Newsletter and logo	Members, but also for general distribution	Serious, formal, factual; gives account	17 May 1992
"	"	Urge members to write letter; address to send appeals to	To get reader to write a letter - instructional	"	"	More willing, pleading	"
Amnesty Int. In Action	"	Members, outreach network groups, campaign methods	To recruit members, persuade and inform	Fact Sheet	Potential members	Appealing	?
"	"	Symbolic events, action used	"	Fact sheet with diagram	"	"	?
Letter to P.M.	Public person	Complaint about Chirac's nuclear tests.	Try to persuade govt into speaking out against nuclear tests. Backed up with info to support cause	Letter	P.M. + govt	Assertive, demanding	6 Sept 1995
Reply to above letter	Secretary	States receipt of letter	To acknowledge letter, inform	Letter	Sender of letter	Blunt, formal, rude, telegraphic	3 Oct 1995
NON!	Greenpeace	Appeal to public to write a protest about nuclear tests	Persuasive, with few facts	Poster / Advert	General public / potential campaigners	urgent, compelling reader to join	95/96
NON!	Greenpeace	Appeals in more detail	Persuasive, with more facts	Letter, ad, info pack	"	"	95/96
Integration makes the difference	John Bold	About methods for teaching kids with Downs Syndrome	To inform favourable. Publicise cause	*Guardian* article (education section)	Teachers, m/c or those interested in education	Reportive, compli-mentary	28 March 1995
Student income falls as grants ⓐ freeze bites	Meikle	Statistics on grants now + future	To inform about past, present and future state	*Guardian* article	UWC / MC students or parents	Factual, critical towards end	29 March 1995
Hardship has got worse ⓑ	Newsome	3 students' views	Inform, persuade against	*Guardian* article	"	Critical / hostile	"
Opportunities after school	Emma Delap	Info on options, how to decide + how to get needs met	Inform, open awareness	Info leaflet	Disabled students 16+ considering future	Simple lang, friendly, chatty	"
Livestock militants ⓐ promise to renew picketing at ports	Michael Hornsby	States actions of police and protestors * Direct Action examples	To inform from a neutral stance	*Times* Article	UWC, public, Tory?	Reporting, factual, balanced	14 April 1995

TITLE	AUTHOR	SUMMARY	PURPOSE	GENRE	AUDIENCE	TONE	DATE
Airport group digs in (b)	"	Actions of animal rights people at Coventry airport	To inform/ persuade	Times Article	"	More pro-reformers P.G.	"
Meetings + Demos (a)	H. Street	States rights of public meetings	Inform and enforce law	Law text book	Students: A-lvl / university	Pro-police	?
Riot & Rout Unlawful assembly	Bennett et al	Definitions	Define protest and rights to arrest	Law text book	Students: A-lvl / university	Pro-police	post 1986
Affray (a)	Berryman	• charge • mode of trial • legal notes + definitions	Inform: pro-law against P.G.s	Magistrates' Court Guide	For students - A level Pol, GCSE Bus Studies + humanities etc	Abrupt, formal	"
Disorderly conduct (b)	"	• charge • legal notes + definitions	Inform: pro-law against P.G.s	Magistrates' Court Guide	"	"	"
A Green Manifesto (See summary there)	Irvine and Ponton	Front cov + blurb - radical syst change to green. Intro: ways to achieve green issues - changes in past - working from within - pressure from outside	To inform + persuade	Book chapter: cover + blurb Picture + text	Intelligent voters interested in the idea of a 'green manifesto'. – politics, social policy, Uni students or A level	Optimistic to green issues	?
Wildlife Magazine	Cox	Editorial – On people who read mag + into environ issues. One writer in P.G.	Entertain, inform and persuade to help wildlife	Editorial column	See p.26	Chatty and friendly	Aug 1995
"	Greenoak + Thomas	Awards for nature writing + winning story	"	Editorial and J Thomas' short story	Wildlife sympathisers	Evocative	"
"	Friends of the Earth	Advertisement	Persuasive, get you to donate money, little info	Advert. Photo, text + donation form	Environment-alists	Pleading	90s

CATEGORIES:

Direct action:
CND → 4,5,3,2.
A. Int → 6, 8.
Greenpeace → 10,11,12,13.
Friends of Earth → 27.
Live Animals → 17.

Opps. to P.G.s
Govt: Brit → 11
         Foreign - 6,9.
Law: 16, 14, 19.
Politics: 24, 22.

Student info:
2,3 → CND.
A. Int → 8.
15 → locus.
16 → Disabled
       opportunities

Public Involvement
CND → 5
A. Int → 7,8,9
Animals → 17
Nuclear tests → 10
Wildlife → 28,26
Doans → 14

Publicity:
Letters: 10, 7,13
Ads → 16,12,13,27
Demos → 5, 17
Articles → 13,15, 14, 17
Leaflets → 16,9,8, 2,3
Magazines → 28,26

In this chapter you have learnt that in preparing for your exam task you should:

- establish the provenance of each text in the source material;
- check for any contradictions or inconsistencies in the source material;
- put the texts into categories;
- make connections between the texts and impose a structure on the material;
- summarise and annotate the texts.

2 Be Conventional

In this chapter, we look carefully at the tasks that examiners set to see exactly what it is they demand of you. We shall look at the features common to every task and then finish by concentrating on the conventions of some of the more common texts that you are required to construct.

Exam conventions

What's the first thing that you do when confronted with an exam paper? Obviously, you look at the questions or tasks you are invited to attempt, but this 'looking-at' can be crucial to your success, because too many candidates merely glance at what they are asked to do and then plunge straight into writing their answers. This approach can lead to potentially disastrous results. Examiners often complain that candidates don't answer the questions set, but instead, write on what they thought was asked. These candidates almost invariably fail. Questions demand just the same careful reading as does the source material.

Look at this task that was set recently. The material that was linked with this question dealt with some of the causes of language change, together with examples of language change in action.

An educational publishing company is launching a range of lively and informative wall posters for display in school classrooms on important topics about the English Language. The posters are aimed at pupils in years 7 and 8 (11–13 year olds).

Each poster will deal with a separate topic. These will include *English as a World Language*, *The History of English* and *A Guide to English Grammar*, for example.

You have been asked to write the text of about 800 words for the poster on *Language Change*, using the material in the source file. You should briefly indicate the layout of your poster and any illustrations that you wish to use.

You'll see from a careful reading of this question that you are being asked to do four things:

1 to write for an *audience* of 11–13 year old school pupils;
2 to *inform* them about language change;
3 to produce the text for *a classroom wall poster*; and
4 to write a text of about *800 words*.

So then, this question identifies:

- the *audience* for the text;
- the *purpose* of the text;
- the *genre (or type)* of text;
- the *length* of the text.

Naturally, each of these requirements will have consequences for the way you construct your new text – the voice you choose, the material you select and the structure you impose, for example. We'll be looking at these things later in the book. For the moment, we'll concentrate on the four elements of the question, as you'll usually find each of them in every task set, whatever syllabus you are following. Sometimes, the task may not specify how long your new text should be, but this is likely to be obvious from its audience, purpose and genre.

ACTIVITY 5

Here are two recent questions. Read them carefully and identify the audience, purpose, genre/type and length (if specified) of each new text.

1 You are a member of a pressure group with strong views about the subject dealt with in the pre-release material. You have been invited by your local radio station to contribute to their one minute Open Opinion programme slot (150–200 words). Write the text of your contribution, using only the material provided. [The pre-release material was about the use of animals in testing for new products, both cosmetic and medical].

2 You are employed by the publicity department of a company which specialises in transferring famous and historic recordings (jazz, popular, classical) to Compact Disc. The company is about to produce a CD catalogue and your department is responsible for editing its contents and supplying one or two articles to interest and attract potential buyers of the company's releases. The company hopes that by arousing interest in the past it will encourage CD buyers to explore earlier recordings that have benefited from transfer to the CD format.

Your task is to write an article on the early days of recorded sound. The editor has restricted you to about 1500 words. You should describe some of the historical circumstances and also provide a simple and interesting explanation of the underlying principles of recorded sound.

You are not expected to trace the history of recorded sound up to the CD or to explain how such discs work, but to confine yourself to the period, the personalities and the inventions described in the file. Above all the piece should be lively and genuinely informative.

We'll be looking at each of these important features of an answer in this chapter, but will be concentrating on the types of text that you may be asked to construct. *Audience* and *Purpose* will be covered in more detail in Chapter 5.

Length

If you are given a task that specifies the number of words you should use in your new text, such as in the *Recorded Sound* assignment, you shouldn't worry if you don't exactly hit the target. You wouldn't be penalised if you used 1099 words in answering a question that required a text of 1100; similarly, if you used 1101, there would be no penalty. Obviously, you need to be sensible: if the task indicates, as many do, '*about* 1100 words', then you are allowed a certain amount of leeway – around 100 words on either side. However, if you considerably over- or under-shoot the target, then you are very likely to lose marks. The reason for this is not primarily that you have used too few or too many words, but that what you have written will be ineffective in achieving its intended purpose. For example, if you had been asked to write the script for an 1100 word illustrated talk to 6 and 7 year olds on the importance of dental hygiene and your script were 1800 words, then you would have given the children too much information. They would become bored and fidgety and would not remember the important parts of your talk. Thus you would not have achieved your purpose. If your talk were far too short then similarly, it would be ineffective, because too much information would have been omitted.

The most important question, then, that you can ask of any new text that you are constructing is 'How effective would my text be?' It's *the* most important, because it's the first one that examiners ask and if the answer is 'not very' or 'not at all', then you should consider some radical rewriting. Obviously, there are many other factors that contribute to the effectiveness of a text and we shall be looking at these later, but sticking closely to the specified number of words is one of the most important and one of the easiest.

It's a good idea therefore to get used to what 100, 200, or 500 words in your own writing looks like so that you can make a rough estimate of how many words you are actually using in your text. Do you know how many words, on average, you write per line? Or per page? Ascertaining the answer should give you an idea of how close you are to hitting the word count target. Remember two things, though:

- your word count could mount rapidly if you rely heavily on using unedited (or cut-out) material from the sources in your own text;
- many of the tasks that you are given will require other types of writing than continuous prose. You should take this into consideration when estimating your word count.

Purpose and audience

Earlier in this chapter it was stressed that the audience you are writing for and the purpose of your text will determine both your selection of material and the voice in which you present this material to the reader (or listener). We are going to take a further brief look at this now.

Below is a short extract from what one student wrote in an examination. She had been asked to write the script for a cassette tape that visitors to the Rodin Museum in Paris could hire to guide them around the works of this great French sculptor. The tape was meant to be lively and informative, giving something of the background to the sculptures and setting them in the context of Rodin's life and achievement. The audience was composed of people who were not familiar with his work and who did not normally visit art galleries and museums. Read the extract carefully.

TEXT 9

As you enter Room B, you will be faced with the 'Gates of Hell'. Rodin started work on the 'Gates' in 1880 and the enormous task occupied and fascinated him for over twenty years. It was never, however, finished as Rodin died before its completion. It was originally intended for the Museum of Decorative Arts and then the old Seminary of St Sulpice in the Place St Sulpice, Paris. His original idea was again connected to Dante and his work 'Inferno'. The only actual groups left taken from Dante's poem are 'Paolo and Francesca' and 'Ugolino'. The poet Baudelaire, the tragic and sensual author of 'Les Fleurs du Mal' also influenced Rodin. The gate today contains 186 figures. On the top of the gate looking down are 'The Three Shadows' as though they are reading the words of the poet there 'Lasciate ogni speranza, o voi ch'entrate'. Below them is 'The Thinker' also contemplating the tragedy. Right at the bottom are the lost women, as Baudelaire conceived them.

How effective would this be in achieving its intended purpose? Probably, not very. So, let's have a look at why this might be the case.

ACTIVITY 6

1 Try reading it aloud. Remember, it is intended to be a script to be listened to, not read. Does the writer use a speaking voice? Is the listener being addressed in a lively and friendly way? Pick out those parts of Text 9 that seem to you to be more suited to the written than the spoken word.

2 Discuss whether too much information has been included for this particular audience. Remember they do not normally visit museums and art galleries.

COMMENTARY

The writer has not thought sufficiently about the circumstances under which her text would be used in the Museum. Firstly, she has chosen to include too much information that could be off-putting to inexperienced visitors. They are told about the Museum of Decorative Arts, the old seminary of St Sulpice in the Place St Sulpice, Dante, Paolo and Francesca, Ugolino, the poet Baudelaire, the tragic and sensual author of *Les Fleurs du Mal* and the writer leaves Dante's Italian untranslated (it means *Abandon hope, all ye who enter here*). Secondly, she has not addressed the visitors in an appropriate speaking voice. Look, for example, at just one sentence:

> *It was never, however, finished as Rodin died before its completion.*

Now compare it with this version:

> *Rodin died before he could finish 'The Gates of Hell'.*

The changes make the sentence easier to speak and therefore to listen to. The changes comprise:

■ a formal word *completion* has been removed and the redundancy of *finished* and *completion* thus overcome;

■ *Rodin* has become the focus of the sentence by becoming its subject, not *it*;

■ *however*, a word more often found in writing than in speech, has been removed;

■ the information has become more specific as *The Gates of Hell* replaces *it*.

These changes, though small, have made it more likely that the audience would listen and the purpose of the tape would thus have been achieved.

ACTIVITY 7

Now that you have seen just what a difference such a small piece of re-drafting can make, re-write the whole of the extract so that it will appeal more to its intended audience.

ACTIVITY 8

Here are two further unaltered short extracts from students' work. The task they were given was to write a booklet on castles for 8–12 year olds that would give the children an exciting and fresh glimpse into another world, but these two extracts are neither exciting nor fresh.

1 Re-write both extracts so that they meet the needs of the audience.
2 Having re-written them you should be in a good position to offer advice to students so that they could avoid similar mistakes in future. List the advice you would give.

TEXT 10
What is a castle?

The Castle was the properly fortified military residence of a lord, and by lord, it included, king, duke, count, and certain kinds of knight.

Buildings are usually designed and constructed for a single purpose. Castles were the exception. From the beginning they were built for two purposes. It was a home for the owner and at the same time it was a structure strong enough to keep unwanted people out.

Many castles were built in Great Britain and were of two designs – the fortified great tower and the fortified enclosure, or a combination of both.

The Great Tower is generally higher than its width, nowadays it is called a 'keep'.

TEXT 11
Storage of arms and armour with the castle

It was said by castle owners 'He who held the castle, controlled the land around it.'

For a lord to keep his castle and the land surrounding the castle, would usually mean having to win battles from rebellious neighbours, and to win battles, arms armour and munition was needed.

It was their duty to make the lord of the castle powerful, and to keep law and order and also to guarantee some preparedness in the event of rebellion or war.

The lords were so particular about the upkeep of their aims, that they made it a specific chore for their workers to maintain it.

The three pieces of re-writing that you have undertaken will have demonstrated just how inextricably interwoven are the audience for, and the purpose of, your new text. These will suggest both the voice(s) you should use to address your audience and the way you should structure and organise the material you select for your new text. They are the subject of the following two chapters.

Text type

Look at these three short texts. Though you probably won't have seen any one of them before, it would be very surprising if you didn't immediately recognise what type of text each was. To allay any lingering doubts you may have, they are:

Text 12 The first page of 'A Parent's Guide to Solvents', a short information booklet published by the Department of Health.
Text 13 A menu from a pub-restaurant
Text 14 A letter from *Just 17's* problem page 'Confidential'

TEXT 12

What is solvent sniffing?

Solvent sniffing usually means getting 'high' by breathing in the fumes from butane, aerosols, glues or other products found around most people's houses or which are easily available from shops. The most common term for this is 'glue sniffing', but there are many other products that can be sniffed:

- butane gas (in cigarette lighters and refill canisters. Butane is also used as a propellant in many aerosols)
- aerosol sprays (virtually any aerosol may be used; hairsprays and pain-relieving sprays are common)
- solvent-based glues (such as Evo-Stik)
- correcting fluids (such as Tipp-Ex)
- dry-cleaning fluids
- the contents of some types of fire extinguishers
- thinners
- petrol

In the average home there are over thirty sniffable products.

TEXT 13

 PARTY TIME CHRISTMAS FAYRE BOXING DAY TO NEW YEARS DAY

Starters

Hot from the Pot - Soup of the Day

Mixed Dippers and Barbecue Sauce Dip
A selection of crispy coated Dippers served with crispy Salad Garnish

Prawn and Tuna Fish Cocktail
Succulent Prawns and Tuna Fish served on a bed of Lettuce topped with Lemon Mayonnaise

Main Course

Lancashire Chicken
Chicken Breast filled with Lancashire Cheese wrapped in Bacon & served with a Mushroom Sauce.

8oz Sirloin Steak
Grilled as you like it & served with either Mushrooms Grilled Onions and Tomato or Red Wine and Mushroom Sauce

Rack of Lamb
Served with Mint Sauce and Gravy

Market Fresh Fillet of Cod
Poached and served with either Prawn sauce or simply served with Parsley Butter and a Lemon wedge

All served with Seasonal Vegetables and Potatoes.

Sweets

Deep Dish Apple Pie
Hot with Custard or cold with fresh whipped Cream or Ice Cream

De Luxe Gateau and fresh Whipped Cream

Traditional Christmas Pudding
With Brandy Sauce or Fresh Cream

Profiteroles
Filled with Brandy flavoured Creme Patissiere.

Followed by freshly brewed Coffee and Mints.

Price includes: Glass of House Wine and Crackers
£10.50 *per adult incl. VAT* **£6.00** *per child incl. VAT*
Reservations are required for New Years Eve and for parties over 4 people at all times. Reservations preferred, but not necessary, for parties up to 4 people, subject to table availability.

TEXT 14

I've never had a snog

Recently I was dumped by this boy from my school. He said that every time he tried to kiss me, I just hugged him instead. Although this is true, I couldn't tell him the real reason: I've never kissed a guy before. Now people at school keep asking me why we broke up, and he keeps telling them to ask me. I just don't know what to say!

Ant & Dec fan

• There's no reason to tell other people why you split up – it's none of their business! Besides, there doesn't need to be a specific reason. Don't let yourself feel as though there's something wrong with you, or let other people say you're inadequate. You aren't. OK, you haven't kissed a boy before. So what? Everyone has to do it for the first time. And far better for you to do it with someone you really trust than some guy who just dumps you because you don't fit his expectations. There's no kissing rule book – it's not a competition. Do what feels right in your own time.

The fact that you could identify what type of text each was and distinguish between them indicates that you are familiar with a very large range of texts. Indeed, you probably never even think about this fact, so used are you to encountering texts as part of your daily life. Take, for example, the different texts that I have read so far today. This chapter is being written at 9.50 on a Monday morning and the texts read up to this time include:

- a broadsheet newspaper;
- a magazine;
- an e-mail;
- a letter from a bank inviting me to change my mortgage;
- a bill;
- a shopping list.

Even this list is not comprehensive and does not include the text for this chapter nor the three that we are considering at the moment. This range of text types is not untypical of what we encounter all the time. At a glance we can usually recognise what text type we are reading and whether we need or want to spend much time with it.

Look at the menu text and examine what its distinguishing features are. In other words, what are the characteristics that this menu shares with other menu texts and which enable us to immediately identify it as *menu*? The most obvious one, of course, is the subject matter: most of the nouns used are to be found within the semantic field of food – *chicken, steak* and *apple pie*, for instance. Menus, however, are not the only text types that use this semantic field: recipes, shopping lists and diet sheets are others. So there must be other features that signal 'menu' to the reader. Amongst these we might note:

- the organisation of the text into three separate sections headed *Starters, Main course* and *Sweets*. This is signalled by the used of italicised headings in larger print;
- most items on the menu are followed by a rather fulsome description. So *Lancashire Chicken* is qualified by *Chicken breast filled with Lancashire cheese wrapped in Bacon and served in a Mushroom sauce*. Again, different fonts are used to signpost this;
- the use of a rather 'clipped' style. So, for example, the writer says *Rack of Lamb Served with Mint Sauce and Gravy*, not *A Rack of Lamb which is Served with Mint Sauce and Gravy*.
- Similarly, *Price includes Glass of House Wine* and not *The Price includes a Glass of House Wine;*
- a distinctive layout which emphasises the text's organisation and structure.

There is more that could be said, particularly about the writer's use of language, but a book in this series, *Language and Style*, will show you in more detail how to identify, describe and evaluate different stylistic features.

ACTIVITY 9

1 In small groups, discuss Texts 13 and 14 and decide what are the features of each that enable you quickly to identify the type it is.
2 For further practice: each member of the class or group should:
   a choose a short text;
   b list its distinguishing characteristics;
   c pass this list of characteristics to other members of the group;
   d ask them to identify the text type just from the list; and
   e see if they were right!

COMMENTARY

We have been concentrating on this, because, as you will remember, every assignment that you are given specifies the text type or genre your new text must be in addition to specifying its audience, purpose and length. Of course, it's unlikely that you would be asked to write a menu, but few text types can be ruled out. In fact, the only one that examiners exclude is the essay. One examination board will *never* ask you to write an essay, though you can be quite sure that some candidates will write one, whatever text type they are asked to produce. Make sure that you aren't the one who writes an essay when you've been asked for a radio script!

Below is a list of the text types you may be asked to write in examinations. It's a very varied list which includes:

radio scripts	short information booklets	'faction' documentaries
wall posters	discussion documents	guide books
reports	theatre programmes	illustrated cards for
anthologies	CD liner notes	inclusion in a breakfast
classroom workpacks	lecture presentations	cereal packet
scripts for pre-recorded tapes	newspaper articles	
	magazine articles	

Even this list isn't comprehensive, but you can see what a range it covers. Of course, future examinations may well ask you to produce other types of text. So, be prepared.

Part of this preparedness is to become as familiar as you can with the conventions of many different types of text. The work you have done so far in this chapter should have shown you what is involved in this.

If you were asked, for example, to write a short information booklet, the examiners expect that you will be aware of the conventions of this genre; if you were asked to write a magazine article, then similarly you need to know its conventions.

We won't be able to cover all the possible text types in this short book and it would be surprising if you were able to do so in your classes, so part of the work for the course that you can do in your own time is to read as many different types of text as you can and to read them purposefully, the purpose being to learn the conventions and communication strategies employed. You'll have noticed, too, the list of text types contains radio scripts, scripts for pre-recorded tapes and lecture presentations. You've already seen one example of this in the work you did on the Rodin passage. Obviously, you will need to ensure you are familiar not only with the conventions of written, but also with those of spoken texts. If all your radio

TEXT 15

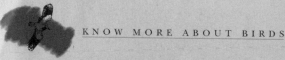

To glimpse a jay ...

Widespread but shy, the jay is a treat to see. With numbers on the increase, it's worth keeping an eye out for this bird of contrasts.

By far the most colourful member of the crow family, the jay is mainly a woodland bird.

Jays are quite common in Britain, but it is rare to get a good view of one. They tend to be most obvious in the autumn when they make regular forays to acorn-laden oak trees to stock up on supplies of their staple food, burying them for a rich winter food source. What usually gives them away are their raucous, grating calls issuing from the undergrowth of a wood or copse, as the birds move about in the shelter of the vegetation. If they do emerge into the open of a woodland glade or clearing, or flit through the canopy, you will be able to recognise them immediately by their bright white rump patch. Jays (*Garrulus glandarius*) are quite large birds – about 34 cm in length, with broad wings – and have a characteristic heavy, undulating flight. On the ground, too, they are fairly ungainly, and tend to jump or bound along, rather than walking or running. In many ways they are contradictory birds – colourful yet surprisingly hard

to spot; bold and aggressive at times yet frequently shy and skulking; harmful to other songbirds yet beneficial in woodland; beautiful but with ugly, grating calls. They are also rather brainy birds. In common with fellow members of the crow family they can adapt quickly to changes in food supply, and also remember well where they have hidden supplies.

WHERE CAN WE FIND JAYS?

Jays are common throughout Europe, except for the far north, and are found right across Asia to Japan and China, as well as North Africa. There are several sub-species, however, each occupying a different area, and each with a slightly different pattern of plumage. The British sub-species is also found in Belgium and the Netherlands, but different races occur in Ireland, Spain and in other parts of Europe and Asia.

In Britain there are an estimated

160,000 pairs, and the numbers have shown a slight increase overall in the last few decades. During the last century, and until World War I, jays, along with their close relatives magpies, were persecuted by gamekeepers because they were seen as major predators of young game birds. This was probably the main factor in keeping the numbers down. In recent years this threat has declined, though the increase in numbers may also be due to the spread of plantations, which have opened up fresh breeding sites.

In Britain, jays are most abundant in the south, spreading roughly as far north as the South Pennines. Further north than this, and in Ireland, they are much more patchily distributed, and are also absent from most of the Fens and from east Lincolnshire. The southern counties of England, notably Kent, Sussex and Hampshire, hold the highest densities of all. In Ireland (which has some 10,000

Jays feed greedily on beech mast, acorns and berries during the autumn. Spare nut food is often collected at this time of abundance and cached for future consumption, aiding dispersal of trees as a result.

JAY FACT FILE

Unlike most other members of the crow family, jays are bright, colourful birds. Male and female are very similar in plumage and are indistinguishable in the field.

The main body colour is pinkish, shading to brownish on the back, with the chin, rump and tail-base being pure white. The tail and flight feathers of the wings are grey-black, contrasting sharply with the white rump, especially in flight.

The stout bill is dark, and there is a broad black moustache on the cheek, below the rather pale eye. A closer look at the bird in flight reveals that each wing covert feather has a repeating sequence of blue, white and black markings.

A striking feature is the crest of black and white feathers on the top of the head, raised in display to other birds or when the bird is otherwise excited.

The jay is easily recognisable as it takes to the air, since no other medium-sized woodland bird flashes a white rump as it flies away.

The jay has a bright pink-buff plumage, surprisingly hard to see in foliage but conspicuous to predators when out in the open.

Each wing has a patch of electric blue feathers at the base of the primary feathers, often clearly visible in flight.

● **NAMES**
English name: Jay
Latin name: *Garrulus glandarius*

● **SIZE**
Length 34 cm; a little larger than a jackdaw, and much paler and more colourful

● **KEY FEATURES**
Shows white rump-patch in flight

● **NEST**
Made from sticks, often low down in a bush or tree

● **EGGS**
5–6 (occasionally 8+), greenish, with brown speckles

● **FOOD**
Opportunist feeders: earthworms, beetles, eggs, nestlings, small mammals, and even other birds, as well as many types of fruit and seeds, including large items such as beech mast and acorns

● **VOICE**
Often makes raucous, rasping calls; quiet song is rarely heard

● **BREEDING**
Incubation 16 days, in March/April

DISTRIBUTION OF JAYS IN THE BRITISH ISLES

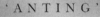

● **YOUNG**
Fledge at about 20 days old

● **HABITAT**
Woodland (especially with oaks), plantations, copses, hedgerows

● **DISTRIBUTION**
Most of Europe, except the far north; concentrated in south and east of Britain but found throughout most of British Isles, except far north and west

'ANTING'

A rather strange habit in which jays occasionally indulge is 'anting'. This is rarely photographed and has only been observed quite recently. The bird sits on an active anthill and spreads out its feathers so that the ants swarm all over its body and among the plumage. The bird seems to benefit from the insecticidal properties of the ants' defensive secretions, which it then spreads through its feathers by preening.

Jays (and the closely related magpie) cause distress amongst bird-lovers because of their habit of robbing the nests of other birds, particularly songbirds, and eating their eggs and young. This jay has found a moorhen nest. Distressing though this sort of predation is, there is little or no evidence to indicate that it has a significant effect on the total numbers of songbirds. Jays certainly kill fewer of our garden birds than domestic cats.

listening is confined to music stations then from time to time you'll need
to tune into those on which the spoken word plays a prominent part, such
as Radios 4 and 5, though these are not the only ones. The reason for this
is, of course, that you can't write a script for a programme whose main
content is musical and in which speech is confined to the unscripted
remarks of the DJ.

We are now going to take a more detailed look at two of the genres, one
written and one spoken, that are frequently set in examinations. We'll
begin by considering the 'part-work'. This, as you will know, is an
illustrated magazine that is published at regular intervals and which builds
up over a substantial number of issues into a comprehensive reference
work. The primary purposes are usually either informative (*Military
Aircraft* or *Great Painters*, for example) or instructional (*Great Dishes of the
World* or *The Complete Home Handyman*).Our example is taken from the
informative part work, *Wildlife of Britain* (Text 15).

The typical features of this part-work are:

■ use of attractive illustrations and maps;
■ a variety of fonts and typesizes used consistently for different functions
  within the text (captions, main text, headlines, for example);
■ logo of a bird in flight to signal a particular section of the magazine
  together with the title 'Know More About Birds';
■ differently shaped texts on the double page spread. The texts can be read
  almost in any order, especially those on the right hand page;
■ a box within a box ('Anting');
■ avoidance of over technical language. Only *Garrulus glandarius* would be
  unfamiliar to the reader and this is glossed;
■ lexis that is suitable for the intelligent, interested reader, but not one
  who is an ornithologist;
■ a relatively formal style, with no idiomatic lexis;
■ left hand page similar to a newspaper with a teaser headline ('To glimpse
  a jay') and a paragraph separate from the main body of the text;
■ text in columns with a subheading to inform readers of the subject
  matter of the following section;
■ further information about the bird given in short captions
  accompanying the photographs;
■ 'Jay Fact File' chops the text up into short informative chunks;
■ bullet points that suggest this pattern (Names, Size, Key Features,
  Nest. . .) which is followed for all birds in the series;
■ bullet point sections written in note form: not <u>*The* habitat *is* woodland</u>
  but *Habitat Woodland*.

You'll have noticed that the writer uses continuous prose as only a part of
his or her communication strategies and that s/he has employed a variety of
other methods to inform (and entertain) the readers. Essay writing does *not*
play any part in the repertoire of strategies at all.

You may have been thinking that it would be very difficult indeed for you
to construct in the examination a text that looked like the *Wildlife in
Britain* extract we have been considering. But, don't worry. You aren't
expected to! The rubric from one board states that 'it is important to

produce at the end of the examination a text that is complete in outline and is sufficiently detailed for an editor or producer to be able to approve it'. In other words, you should concentrate on writing a text that an editor thinks would achieve its purpose. In the real world, as opposed to the world of examinations, having selected your text for publication, the editor would then employ graphic designers and picture editors to work with your text and produce the finished article. Of course, your 'text', as in the *Wildlife in Britain* example, might very well consist of a number of short texts that go to make up your complete answer.

You are therefore required only to write *the text*. After all, it *is* an English Language not an Art or Graphics examination you are sitting. Sometimes the question might ask you to suggest a layout for your text if this is going to form an integral part of the final publication. In this case, all you need do is to provide a plan of what you would like the piece to look like. Here's an example:

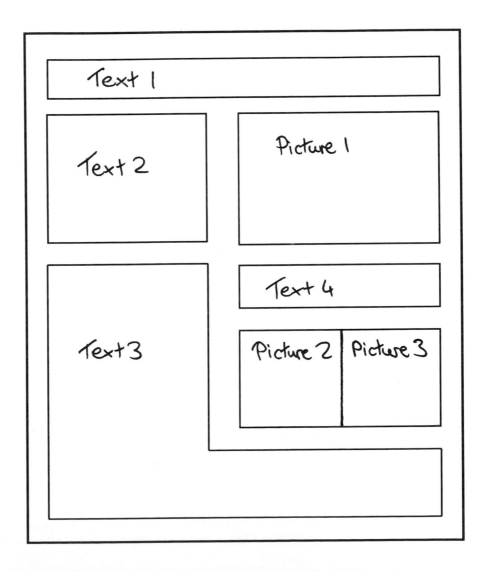

If you label each section of your text clearly in your plan, as in the example, and then label each corresponding part of your written answer, the examiner (or editor) will have no problems in understanding what you intended and, of course, would be able to give the graphic designer some clear instructions. You don't have to go into a lot of detail, but your sketch plan must be clear.

Spoken texts

So far in this chapter we have looked at written texts, but, as we saw, you need to be familiar with the conventions of spoken texts as well, if you are to be fully prepared for what you may be asked to produce in these examinations. So our focus will now shift to the radio script, a text type that you are frequently asked to write, but not, you'll remember, the only spoken type required. Talks are sometimes requested.

The best way to familiarise yourself with the conventions of radio scripts is, of course, to listen to as many different programmes as you can. Remember, as we said earlier, the emphasis should be on the spoken word, but this does not mean that the programme should be either a monologue or one that uses none of the array of technical resources that are available to radio producers. There are many types of spoken word programme and a recent issue of *Radio Times* reveals the following selection from just two days' schedule:

- Talks (*Letter from America;* a writer, Charles Handy retraces his childhood);
- Documentaries on contemporary issues (*The Indian General Election; Islamic Fundamentalism*);
- Magazine programmes containing a variety of items (*The Food Programme; Medicine Now*);
- Original plays;
- A biographical programme recreating the life of a poet (George Mackay Brown);
- A dramatisation of a novel (John Wyndham's 'The Kraken Wakes');
- An anthology of readings from letters from soldiers in World War I together with a linking commentary.

There were others featuring the spoken word: interviews, discussion programmes and phone-ins, for example. These are, however, of no use to us because they are all impromptu and therefore by their very nature need little, if any, scripting, only a running order. You can't write a script for a phone-in, though many candidates do try to do so! You can see from this selection of programmes that you may need to broaden your radio experience if Radio 1 or Key 103, for example, form the bulk of your listening.

To give you an idea of the variety of content and of the different techniques of presentation in just one short radio programme, here is a summary of what it contained. The programme is called *On These Days*, lasts for just 15 minutes and was broadcast daily on Radio 4. It looked at various aspects of life 50 years ago and this particular programme concentrated on the impact of the controversial American Dr Kinsey and his investigations into human sexual behaviour. The programme contained:

- the title and closing credits read by a continuity announcer;
- extracts from period songs and music to set the mood and provide comment on the content of the programme;
- extracts from *The Kinsey Report* read in an American accent;
- edited comments from some of the men and women to whom Kinsey spoke when conducting his research;
- comments from modern experts on sexual behaviour;
- comment from an 'agony aunt';
- recordings of Kinsey himself in 1949;
- edited interviews with five English people recounting their ignorance of sexual matters even in their late teens and early 20s;
- theme music, sound effects and dialogue from the late 1940s British film *Brief Encounter* which was about a passionate (and unconsummated) extra-marital love affair;
- comments on the film from a film historian and critic.

All these were linked by the programme's presenter who gave some historical background material, comments and occasionally named the expert contributors. There were various techniques used including:

- voice over music;
- sound effects;
- fade ins and fade outs to link different sections of the programme;
- cross fades.

In all, there were around 32 separate items that were woven together to construct what was, remember, only a 15 minute programme. You can work out for yourself the average length of each piece, but some lasted for only a few seconds. You should also be able to see the similarity with what you are asked to do. This weaving together of separate items is *exactly* what you are doing when you are constructing your new texts in this part of the English Language course.

ACTIVITY 10

These were the conventions and techniques of just one type of radio programme. Each member of the group or class should listen carefully to a different type and compile a similar list. Remind yourself of the list on p 28. Your lists should consist of:

1 all the separate items that constitute the whole programme; and

2 the different techniques employed. Remember to choose a programme in which the scripted spoken voice predominates. By comparing lists, you should then have a comprehensive catalogue on which to draw if you are asked to write your own programme script.

ACTIVITY 11

The following passage is part of the opening of Dickens' 19th century novel *Great Expectations* in which the young Philip Pirrip (Pip) is surprised by the escaped convict, Magwitch. The scene is set in a graveyard near the marshes of the Thames Estuary. Write the script for a radio dramatisation of this episode. Try not to rely overmuch, if at all, on a narrator. You should aim to make your dramatisation last about five minutes, so you will also have to employ your skills of selection, adaptation and précis.

TEXT 16

My father's family name being Pirrip, and my Christian name Philip, my infant tongue could make of both names nothing longer or more explicit than Pip. So, I called myself Pip, and came to be called Pip.

Ours was the marsh country, down by the river, within, as the river wound, twenty miles of the sea. My first most vivid and broad impression of the identity of things, seems to me to have been gained on a memorable raw afternoon towards evening. At such a time I found out for certain, that this bleak place overgrown with nettles was the churchyard; and that Philip Pirrip, late of this parish, and also Georgiana wife of the above, were dead and buried; and that Alexander, Bartholomew, Abraham, Tobias, and Roger, infant children of the aforesaid, were also dead and buried; and that the dark flat wilderness beyond the churchyard, intersected with dykes and mounds and gates, with scattered cattle feeding on it, was the marshes; and that the low leaden line beyond, was the river; and that the distant savage lair from which the wind was rushing, was the sea; and that the small bundle of shivers growing afraid of it all and beginning to cry, was Pip.

'Hold your noise!' cried a terrible voice, as a man started up from among the graves at the side of the church porch. 'Keep still, you little devil, or I'll cut your throat!'

A fearful man, all in coarse gray, with a great iron on his leg. A man with no hat, and with broken shoes, and with an old rag tied round his head. A man who had been soaked in water, and smothered in mud, and lamed by stones, and cut by flints, and stung by nettles, and torn by briars; who limped, and shivered, and glared and growled; and whose teeth chattered in his head as he seized me by the chin.

'Oh! Don't cut my throat, sir,' I pleaded in terror. 'Pray don't do it, sir.'

'Tell us your name!' said the man. 'Quick!'

'Pip, sir.'

'Once more,' said the man, staring at me. 'Give it mouth!'

'Pip. Pip, sir.'

'Show us where you live,' said the man. 'Pint out the place!'

I pointed to where our village lay, on the flat in-shore among the alder-trees and pollards, a mile or more from the church.

The man, after looking at me for a moment, turned me upside-down, and emptied my pockets. There was nothing in them but a piece of bread. When the church came to itself – for he was so sudden and strong that he made it go head over heels before me, and I saw the steeple under my feet – when the church came to itself, I say, I was seated on a high tombstone, trembling, while he ate the bread ravenously.

'You young dog,' said the man, licking his lips, 'what fat cheeks you ha' got.'

I believe they were fat, though I was at that time undersized for my years, and not strong.

'Darn me if I couldn't eat 'em,' said the man, with a threatening shake of his head, 'and if I han't half a mind to 't!'

I earnestly expressed my hope that he wouldn't, and held tighter to the tombstone on which he had put me; partly to keep myself upon it; partly, to keep myself from crying.

'Now then, lookee here!' said the man. 'Where's your mother?'

'There, sir!' said I.

He started, made a short run, and stopped and looked over his shoulder.

'There, sir!' I timidly exclaimed. '"Also Georgiana." That's my mother.'

'Oh!' said he, coming back. 'And is that your father alonger your mother?'

'Yes, sir,' said I; 'him too; late of this parish.'

'Ha!' he muttered then, considering. 'Who d' ye live with – supposin' you're kindly let to live, which I han't made up my mind about?'

'My sister, sir – Mrs Joe Gargery – wife of Joe Gargery, the blacksmith, sir.'

'Blacksmith, eh?' said he. And looked down at his leg.

After darkly looking at his leg and at me several times, he came closer to my tombstone, took me by both arms, and tilted me back as far as he could hold me; so that his eyes looked most powerfully down into mine, and mine looked most helplessly up into his.

'Now lookee here,' he said, 'the question being whether you're to be let to live. You know what a file is?'

'Yes, sir.'

'And you know what wittles is?'

'Yes, sir.'

After each question he tilted me over a little more, so as to give me a greater sense of helplessness and danger.

'You get me a file.' He tilted me again. 'And you get me wittles.' He tilted me again. 'You bring 'em both to me.' He tilted me again. 'Or I'll have your heart and liver out.' He tilted me again.

I was dreadfully frightened, and so giddy that I clung to him with both hands, and said, 'If you would kindly please to let me keep upright, sir, perhaps I shouldn't be sick, and perhaps I could attend more.'

He gave me a most tremendous dip and roll, so that the church jumped over its own weather-cock. Then, he held me by the arms, in an upright position on the top of the stone, and went on in these fearful terms:

'You bring me, to-morrow morning early, that file and them wittles. You bring the lot to me, at that old Battery over yonder. You do it, and you never dare to say a word or dare to make a sign concerning your having seen such a person as me, or any person sumever, and you shall be let to live. You fail, or you go from my words in any partickler, no matter how small it is, and your heart and your liver shall be tore out, roasted and ate. Now, I ain't alone, as you may think I am. There's a young man hid with me, in comparison with which young man I am a Angel. That young man hears the words I speak. That young man has a secret way pecooliar to himself, of getting at a boy, and at his heart, and at his liver. It is in wain for a boy to attempt to hide himself from that young man. A boy may lock his door, may be warm in bed, may tuck himself up, may draw the clothes over his head, may think himself comfortable and safe, but that young man will softly creep and creep his way to him and tear him open. I am a keeping that young man from harming of you at the present moment, with great difficulty. I find it wery hard to hold that young man off your inside. Now, what do you say?'

ACTIVITY 12

Radio 4 is broadcasting a series of very short programmes about the smaller islands in the British Isles. Each programme will be a snapshot of the island in question whose aim is to give a sense of its atmosphere and uniqueness, as well as providing facts. Write the script of about 300 words for the programme on St Kilda, basing your answer on the following text by Derek Cooper. *(Question adapted from one set by Edexcel in 1996).*

TEXT 17

Until 29 August 1930 St Kilda was the remotest inhabited island in Britain. When I circumnavigated it aboard the 14,000-ton Uganda, on a National Trust tour of the northern isles, the huge ship was plunging like a toy duck in the turbulent waters of a Force 10 gale despite its stabilisers and massive bulk. Rolling in the enormous seas, we stood off Hirta as giant waves crashed against the tallest and most dramatic sea cliffs in Europe.

Nowhere round offshore Britain is there another sight like this. Here is the largest gannetry in the world, an outpost of ocean wildlife without equal, a sight to dazzle bird-watchers: 100,000 pairs of puffins, 40,000 pairs of fulmars, 20,000 pairs of guillemots, 12,000 pairs of kittiwakes. There are shearwaters and petrels in abundance, razorbills, gulls, shags and skuas.

It was the birds that enabled man to keep a foothold on St Kilda for some 2,000 years. Corn could be grown, hay made and sheep and cattle kept, but it was the flesh and eggs of sea-birds that provided the staple diet. For a large part of the year mountainous seas would cut the islanders off from the rest of the world. Passing boats might heave to, but time and again landing was impossible.

During the summer in Victorian times, tourists from Oban would occasionally, on a calm day, come ashore to patronise the natives and photograph them, much as you might visit the zoo on a Sunday afternoon. The St Kilda parliament, the daily meeting when tasks for the day were discussed if seldom executed; the skill and daring of the St Kildan fowlers who at the turn of the century were slaughtering 12,000 birds a year; the appalling toll of infant mortality brought about by tetanus infantum; the rigours and hardships of St Kildan life, became a subject of universal curiosity.

The islanders themselves, with little immunity to infection, were prone to the 'boat-cold'. Visitors brought diseases which would sweep through Village Bay and prostrate the island for weeks. It was a close-knit, inbred society without money, without a doctor, without any of the amenities which had become necessities on the mainland. The island was owned by the Macleod of Macleod who lived in distant Skye and the St Kildans relied completely on his beneficence. Annually the factor came to take away fulmars' oil, feathers, salted sea-birds, fish, sheep and tweed, and in return he brought the seed and supplies needed for survival.

By the end of the Great War the St Kildan population had declined to less than 40, of whom many were elderly. The average weekly income of each family was about 10 shillings and it was apparent to the very competent nurse, Williamina Barclay, that it was really only a matter of time before everyone would have to leave. But where would they go? Who would assume responsibility for them?

The winter of 1929–30 was disastrous, there was hunger in every family. On 10 May the missionary, with the approval of his fellow islanders, wrote a petition to the Government that they be evacuated and resettled elsewhere. Several of the abler men had already decided to seek employment on the mainland; that meant that all would have to go. The petition was passed to the skipper of the first trawler that called at the island.

Then the dilemma of the islanders was dramatically highlighted by the death from tuberculosis of 21-year-old Mary Gillies. The lighthouse vessel Hesperus was unable to land a boat to take her off and no doctor could reach her. Despite devoted nursing by Miss Barclay she died on 21 June. It was an event which sealed the fate of St Kilda.

On the morning of 29 August 1930 the Fishery Protection vessel Harebell and the ancient steamer Dunara Castle were moored in Village Bay with steam up ready to complete the evacuation.

The day before had been spent ferrying out personal possessions; the sheep had been taken off. At eight o'clock anchors were weighed; one or two of the old people openly wept. 'The loneliest of Britain's island dwellers', wrote Alasdair Alpin Macgregor who witnessed the evacuation, 'have resigned their heritage to the ghosts and the sea-birds; and the curtain is rung down on haunted homes and the sagas of the centuries.' Strong stuff! But it was the very moving end of an incredible story of endurance on the edge of the world.

Fifty years later the Army maintains a presence on St Kilda, assisted by an oil-fired power-station, frozen food, helicopters and landing craft. In their million-pound missile-tracking station they are on St Kilda but not of it. The island archipelago – Hirta, Soay, Boreray and Dun with its attendant skerries and inaccessible stacks – remains the most sensational piece of offshore archaeology in Britain. In storm force winds, lonely in the waste of the Atlantic, St Kilda is a spectacle that reduces one to silence.

(From Island Britain – Peter Crookston (1993))

In this chapter you have learnt how to read an examination question and the importance of:

- writing appropriately for the specified audience of your new text;
- writing appropriately for the specified purpose of your new text;
- adhering to the specified word count of your new text;
- being familiar with the conventions of a variety of texts and genres.

3 Are You Well Structured?

I n this chapter you will learn how important it is to plan and structure your writing. You will learn about textual coherence – the movement of ideas through a text.

TEXT 18

Cover with foil and bake in the oven for 10–15 minutes. Remove the foil and bake for a further 5–10 minutes until golden brown.

1 pink grapefruit, peeled and segmented, reserving juice.

Serves 3–4

Lay the mackerel fillets skin side down. Season with citrus pepper and salt.

4 spring onions, sliced.

MACKEREL WITH GRAPEFRUIT AND SPRING ONION

Spoon any excess onion and grapefruit around the fish. Pour over the reserved grapefruit juice.

Preheat oven to 190°C/375°F, Gas Mark 5

6 × 6oz (175g) mackerel fillets

Serve the mackerel with seasonal vegetables and sliced, boiled potatoes.

citrus pepper **or** pepper and 1 teaspn (5ml) grated lemon rind

salt

Arrange the grapefruit segments and spring onions on top of each mackerel fillet. Roll up and place in an ovenproof dish.

ACTIVITY 14

1 There's something gone wrong here! You'll have recognised this as a recipe, but one whose constituent parts appear in the wrong order.
   a On your own, reassemble the parts into what you think is the correct order.
   b Discuss with a partner how you reached your decision.
2 Here's a slightly trickier passage for you to re-arrange. It's the text of an advertisement for a limited-edition porcelain statuette of the famous Australian cricketer, Sir Donald Bradman. There are eight paragraphs and if you need to check your version against the original, then turn to the end of the chapter. Again, discuss with a partner how you reached your decision.

A Alas, two balls after taking guard the great man was on the way back to the Pavilion, bowled by the Warwickshire spinner Eric Hollies for 0. His run tally stopped at 6,996, 29 centuries, 13 fifties, 12 Test innings above 200 and a reputation for tearing attacks apart with devastating thoroughness that had become legend.

B Don Bradman – 'The Don' – was born on August 27, 1908, destined to become the greatest batsman of all time, the greatest gatherer of runs, the most magnificent setter of records, a batsman feared by the opposition every time he took guard.

C At 30 his phenomenal run of success was halted by the Second World War. Without that seven year break Bradman might well have set a run-scoring record never to be beaten. As it was he had to settle for another unbeatable target – an all-time Test average of 99.94.

D At the age of 24 he was the target of a new-style attack – 'bodyline' – Douglas Jardine's leg-theory. At 26 he'd scored his second Test triple century. At 28 he led his country for the first time, and was never to lose a rubber.

E No player, before or since, has matched Sir Don's outstanding record with the bat and few have

matched his leadership success either – 24 tests as captain, 15 wins and only three defeats.

F The slight figure from Bowral scored a century on his debut for New South Wales at the age of 19. A year later he had scored 300 runs in an innings for the first time. A year after that he had passed that staggering milestone for his country against England.

G India, South Africa and the West Indies all suffered under the Bradman hammer but none of them so much as England who faced him 37 times in Tests. He gathered 5,028 runs in those 37 matches, amassed 19 centuries and twice raced past 300, on both occasions at Leeds.

H When, at the age of 40, Bradman walked to the Oval wicket for his last Test innings, he and the thousands in the ground who gave him a standing ovation all the way to the crease knew he only needed to score four runs to average 100.00.

COMMENTARY You probably found that some of the following helped you to reorder the two texts:

- your knowledge of textual conventions. Recipes usually have a set order or structure: (i) the name of the dish, (ii) a list of ingredients (often in the order in which they are to be used), (iii) the steps you have to follow to prepare and cook the dish, (iv) serving suggestions and (v) the number of servings that the dish will provide.
- your contextual and lexical knowledge (in this case, of cooking). You couldn't, for example, 'spoon any excess onion and grapefruit around the fish' without previously having arranged these items 'on top of each mackerel fillet'. Only when you had completed the first task might you have any 'excess'.
- other signals and signposts that the writer has provided to indicate the structure of the text and thus guide you through it.

In the Bradman passage there are obviously the dates and ages that have been included in five out of the eight paragraphs. This makes it easy to decide on the order both for these five and for paragraph A, but it is slightly more difficult with paragraphs E and G as there are no such signals. In fact, these two paragraphs could have been slotted in as paragraphs two and three in an alternative revision of the text.

You may have found that the recipe text was easier to re-order than the Bradman. The reason for this, of course, is that recipes usually have a 'given' structure. All recipes follow a very similar order with the result that once you are familiar with one, whether it be Delia Smith's, Mrs Beeton's or your parents', you can predict what the structure of almost any other recipe is going to be. This makes it relatively easy for recipe writers although there is plenty of room for individual stylistic variation within the genre and register. You wouldn't mistake Delia Smith's style for Keith Floyd's, although they are both writing in the recipe genre and register. There are many other types of text that have a 'given' structure that their writers usually follow. If they deviate from the norm it is usually because they want to draw attention to (or 'foreground') particular aspects of their text. So, for example, it is conventional for a preacher to begin his or her sermon with a biblical verse or verses, thus signalling to the congregation (or 'addressees', to use a linguistic term) that this verse will form the basis for the ensuing sermon. If, however, the sermon does not commence in this way, then a congregation used to such a conventional structure may well pay more attention to the sermon than they normally would. Or, at least to its beginning! Conventions, however, cannot be broken too frequently or they would cease to be conventions.

ACTIVITY 14

There are many types of text that have a 'given' structure: for example, menus, lonely-hearts advertisements, sonnets, problem page letters and replies, Sherlock Holmes stories and weather forecasts. Discuss with a partner the text types that you could add to this list of examples.

COMMENTARY

The Bradman text did not have a pre-ordained structure in the way that the recipe did. This means, then, that its writer had to decide for himself in what order to put the material. Now, with this particular text, the task would not have been too difficult, as basically the chronology of Bradman's life provides its structure. Nonetheless the writer had at some stage to make these decisions. The process involved in writing the Bradman text will have been similar to the one involved when you write your English Language exam answer. The similarities are as follows: both you and the Bradman author will have:

- had to read source material on your subject;
- decided which parts of it are relevant to your purpose and audience;
- discarded other parts;
- decided the order in which the material is to appear in the finished piece;
- begun to construct your new text.

If a text does not have a coherent structure then a reader or listener would find it extremely difficult to follow. To encounter a text, whether written or spoken, for the first time can be a daunting experience and the writer attentive to the needs of his/her audience will provide them with enough signposts to ensure that their journey through the text will be an easy one. We'll be looking at signposts in Chapter 4. Of course, it isn't just texts that require structures. Imagine a football match that was played without the structure of two 45 minute halves. All those features that add to the appeal of the game would be lost if the agreed structure were abandoned: the pattern of the game; the opportunity to put things right in the second half following a disastrous first one; the increase in tension as the 90th minute approached with your team desperately hanging on to a 1–0 lead.

Everything that is designed and planned needs a clear structure if it is to be successful and achieve its purpose: buildings, clothes, music, boats, mathematical equations and paintings, for example. Our appreciation of a painting, of a piece of music or even of an equation is considerably diminished if they appear formless and chaotic. We must, however, be careful not to condemn paintings, music or equations at first sight if they appear to us formless or chaotic. It might be, of course, that we cannot yet perceive its underlying organisation. Buildings and boats would be useless and dangerous if they had no coherent design and structure. So it should be very clear from these examples that these things are of paramount importance; texts are no exception to this rule. The activities that you undertook at the start of this chapter should have alerted you to two things:

1 that we can recognise the absence of structure in a text; and
2 that this absence can render a text almost impossible to comprehend.

We are now going to examine a small number of texts to see how they have been structured by their authors. You'll recall that you have already looked at a number of texts – menus, recipes and the jay text (pp 24–25) where structure was very transparent. The next ones do not have a 'given' structure. The first is taken from a booklet issued by the NSPCC. Read it carefully and then look at the outline of its structure that follows the passage.

TEXT 19

Why do parents neglect their children?

If children are to develop and grow into healthy and happy people they need food, warmth, shelter and love. These basic needs are normally met by parents, or other adult caregivers who take on the parental role. Children are vulnerable and completely dependent on their parents to meet their needs. Children can be neglected because their parents put their own interests first or because their parents are having to cope with difficult experiences such as divorce or bereavement.

Sometimes parents neglect their children because they have severe problems of their own such as alcohol or drug abuse. Whatever the reason, parents who fail to make their children's needs the first priority and to ensure their children are safe, warm and properly fed are neglecting those children. Equally children are neglected if those caring for them do not make sure they have enough time to rest, learn and play, or if they fail to show them the love and affection all children need.

Parents ignore their children's needs for many different reasons. Parents who haven't been loved or properly looked after by their own parents are more likely than others to neglect their own children. Social disadvantage can also make neglect more likely. Inadequate housing does not make child-rearing any easier and it can be demoralising. Sometimes there is not enough money to pay the bills for heating and the rent. Sometimes there's not even enough money to buy food for the children. Not having enough money to buy your children new clothes or even a birthday present can be depressing and can undermine a parent's confidence.

Problems can also be made worse by unemployment. It can be very difficult to adjust to life on a greatly reduced income. And unemployment can put a great strain on a relationship. When the main bread-winner – usually the father – loses his job, it's common for him to feel that he's not fulfilling his duties as a husband and father.

If the parents' relationship with each other is unhappy, the children often suffer as well. Even when there is no physical violence parents who constantly row in front of their children are ignoring the children's emotional needs.

Bringing up children without the support of a partner can be hard. Unsupported single parents, and parents who are no longer loved or respected by their partner, do not always have the support they need. Neglect can start, too, if a child's birth was not planned or wanted – or when the pregnancy or birth has been difficult. Not only will a mother feel physically exhausted and find it difficult to cope fully with the needs of a child – particularly the emotional needs – but she might also find it difficult to feel any real affection for her child.

COMMENTARY

- The **title** *Why do parents neglect their children?* poses a question that will be answered in the subsequent paragraphs;
- **Paragraphs 1 and 2** introduce the topic of child neglect by establishing the general point that children have basic needs normally met by parents but that, in contrast, some children are neglected by their parents for a variety of reasons;
- **Paragraphs 3–6** then give specific reasons for child neglect, thus linking back to the title and exemplifying the more general points made in the first two paragraphs. These specific reasons are:

  paragraph 3   the parents themselves having been neglected as children
  inadequate housing
  lack of money
  paragraph 4   unemployment
  paragraph 5   an unhappy relationship between the parents
  paragraph 6   being a single parent or an unloved partner
  an unplanned pregnancy or a difficult birth.

The writer has thus structured the material very clearly and has made it easy for the attentive reader to follow and understand the text.

ACTIVITY 15

1 In pairs, analyse each of the following three texts. For each text, you should agree what the underlying structure is.
2 Discuss your findings with the class or group as a whole.

TEXT 20
The army

The British Expeditionary Force of 1916 was one of the most remarkable and admirable military formations ever to have taken the field, and the Fourth and Third Armies, which were to attack the Somme, provided a perfect cross-section of the sort of units which composed it. Four of the thirteen attacking divisions were regular, were wholly or largely formed, that is, of long-service volunteer soldiers. The 4th Division demonstrated what type of formation this was. All its twelve battalions of fighting infantry were old-sweat units, two Irish, one Scottish, five Midland or North Country, two West Country, one East Anglian, one London; and, despite continuous action since the Battle of Mons in August 1914 many of their experienced pre-war officers and NCOs still survived. The 7th and 8th Divisions were less completely regular, containing as each did a war-raised 'Kitchener' brigade (three brigades of four battalions made a division) but were distinctively regular in spirit. This was true, too, of the 29th Division, which contained two war-raised units – the so-called Public Schools Battalion and the Newfoundland Regiment – but was composed otherwise of the toughest old-sweat battalions, those which had been overseas on imperial garrison duty in August 1914. Three of the 'Kitchener' divisions also contained regular battalions, the 21st, 30th and 32nd, having one in each of its brigades; the rest of their infantry, like all that in the 18th, 31st, 34th and 36th Divisions, was 'Kitchener' or 'New Army'. What made these battalions – 97 out of the 143 destined for the attack – so worthy of note?

First, that they were formed of volunteers. The regular battalions were also raised by voluntary enlistment, but the impulsion which drove a pre-war civilian to join up for 'seven and five' – seven years with the colours, five on the reserve – was most often that of simple poverty. 'I would rather bury you than see you in a red coat' were the words his mother wrote to William Robertson, a ranker who became a field-marshal, on hearing of his enlistment, and they tell us all we need to know about what a respectable Victorian working-class family felt at a son joining the army. Almost any other sort of employment was thought preferable, for soldiering meant exile, low company, drunkenness or its danger, the surrender of all chance of marriage – the removal, in short, of every gentle or improving influence upon which the Victorian poor had been taught to set such store. It is against this background that we must review the extraordinary enthusiasm to enlist which seized the male population of the British Isles in the autumn of 1914 and provided the army, in a little under six months, with nearly two million volunteer soldiers.

(From *The Face of Battle*, John Keegan)

TEXT 21

THE NEW VOLVO 850 TURBO DIESEL. AN INCREDIBLE RATE OF NOTS

Not slow: 0–60mph in 9.9 seconds. Not sluggish: delivers 140bhp. Not dull: capable of 125mph. Not boring: 215lb/ft torque for swift overtaking. Not thirsty: 64mpg at a constant 56mph. Not smoky: lean burn catalytic converter. Not heavy handed: has all the classic Volvo 850 driving characteristics. Not beyond reach: prices start at £21,975. Not your ordinary diesel. THE NEW VOVLO 850TDI. A CAR YOU CAN BELIEVE IN.

TEXT 22

Precision and accuracy

Every day there arise occasions when we have to explain or describe things. To be able to do so precisely and accurately, without losing ourselves in a maze of words, is an accomplishment that saves not only time but frequently money also. At one time or another everyone of us has been bewildered and delayed by the confusing directions of would-be helpers. Some folk are incapable even of directing a stranger to a nearby street.

But let us not be over-critical. We may be no better ourselves. Without practice, it is not too easy to explain or describe even familiar objects or incidents clearly and fully yet concisely. It is difficult to know where to begin, how much to say and, perhaps even more important, how much to leave out.

But, the impatient reader may exclaim, this is a lesson on writing, yet everything you have said so far refers to the spoken word, not to the written. That is true; but our method has been chosen quite deliberately. The tendency to confusion or hesitation in giving spoken directions to which so many of us are liable may be very largely overcome by constant practice in putting down our thoughts on paper. Such practice forms one of the finest exercises imaginable in right thinking. There are indeed people who deliberately evade setting things down on paper. We all know the man who keeps all his accounts, orders and engagements 'in his head'; we know, too, the man who never commits himself to writing because, as the old tag says, 'The written word remains'.

It does, but happily in more senses than one. What you have written down can remain to convict you beyond denial of inaccuracy or muddleheadedness, but it can also stand as friend and saviour when memory has failed or excitement inhibits the faculties. For most of us the written word is far more often friend than foe.

By way of testing this try your hand at one of the subjects given below. Imagine you are without warning called upon to give a clear brief explanation to a friend. Give this explanation first by word of mouth. Then write it down.

1 How to lay a stair-carpet.
2 How to fill a spool for a sewing machine.
3 How to iron a shirt.
4 How to get to the nearest fire station.
5 How to prune a rose garden.
6 The duties of a half-back in Association football.

When you have done your writing, check it over to make certain (a) that you have omitted no essential point, (b) that you have made every point quite clear, and (c) that you have enumerated the steps in the right order.

(From *Good English How to Speak and Write It. A Complete Course of 10 Sections* (Daily Herald, 1935))

Coherence and cohesion

These two terms used in language study are sometimes confused, not surprisingly because they are, in fact, quite closely connected. What you have been mainly working on so far in this chapter is *textual coherence* and you will be looking at *cohesion* very closely in Chapter 4. So what *is* coherence in a text? You have learnt how important it is for any text to have an overall shape or structure and you have already examined this in a number of specific texts. What you have been doing, in other words, is looking at the text's coherence. Coherence, then, is the way that a text, be it spoken or written, is perceived to 'hang together' rather than just being a set of unrelated sentences or utterances. A text would not be fully satisfactory to a listener or a reader if the ideas, concepts or events that it referred to were not consistent with the overall subject matter of the text. So, for example, if the NSPCC text suddenly began speaking of the need to subsidise public transport or even of cruelty to animals or the John Keegan text suddenly began speaking of the Battle of Agincourt rather than that of the Somme, the texts could be accused of incoherence. They would face the same charge if the order or structure of the content of the text were not clear, as in the jumbled recipe or Bradman texts. So, coherence then is the way that the writer or speaker moves his or her ideas through a text. To be successful, a text *must* be coherent.

It follows, therefore, that you must ensure that any text you construct for this part of your examination course must be coherent if it is to be successful. If you are a writer of texts, as you are, then you have to be a writer of coherent ones. If you are following a syllabus that allows you to prepare the material on which your text will be based before you go into the examination, then you will already have begun to impose some structure on it, as we saw in Chapter 1. Prior to the examination itself you will have made links between texts, compared and contrasted others and tried out a variety of possible orders in which you could put the material. However, it is when you are faced with the assignment itself that you must finally decide on a coherent structure for your text. This should be your first task in the examination hall. Don't rush to put pen to paper before you have spent some time planning the shape of your text to be. Resist the impulse to begin writing as soon as you sit down. Inevitably, answers that are produced like this gain a low mark. Reflection and planning should be your first move, not writing. The only writing you should be engaged on is that which is involved in organising and planning the structure of your text, ensuring that it 'hangs together', that it coheres.

Remember that the structure you finally decide upon will be a major contributor to the effectiveness of your text, provided that you stick to it throughout your writing. You shouldn't leave your readers (or listeners) in a fog because they cannot clearly see the direction you are taking. Remember too, that examiners are first and foremost readers and therefore they will be bringing their expectations as readers to your answer, when they encounter it for the first time. So examiners need to assure themselves that the text is coherent. They want to see that you are firmly in control and are guiding them on their journey through the text.

Don't worry that examiners will have at the back of their minds an ideal structure for the text that they are reading and that if your text fails to match this notional structure then marks will be lost. This simply isn't the case. No examiner will have a preferred shape or structure for a text; the only preference held is that there *must* be a structure and that it should be clear to the reader or listener. Examiners are constantly pleased that candidates find new, unexpected and effective ways of organising their texts and such candidates are duly rewarded. Here are some of the questions that an examiner will ask of the text he/she is reading:

- Is it coherently structured?
- Does it seem to be going somewhere?
- Has the candidate's selection of material been guided by a principle?
- Has the candidate kept the task clearly in mind throughout the script?

If the answer to these four questions about your script is 'Yes', then you are on the way to a good mark.

ACTIVITY 16

Obviously there isn't the space here to give you lots of examples of candidates' answers so you could judge whether an examiner would say 'yes' to the four questions above. So, we're going to look at the plans that candidates made before they began to construct their texts. Remember, though, that some weaker candidates don't plan or structure their responses at all, but plunge straight into their writing. Read each of the plans carefully and discuss with a partner your answers to the following questions:

- Is the plan clear and easy to follow?
- What structure has the writer imposed on the material?
- Is this structure likely to be effective in meeting the demands of the task?
- What advice, if any, would you give to the writer?

A suggested response to the first plan is given for you.

The first two plans were preparing for the task that we have already looked at in Chapter 2. You'll remember that students had been asked to write the text for a 600 word wall poster on Language Change for display in school classrooms. The posters were aimed at pupils in Years 7 and 8 (11–13 year olds).

Plan 1

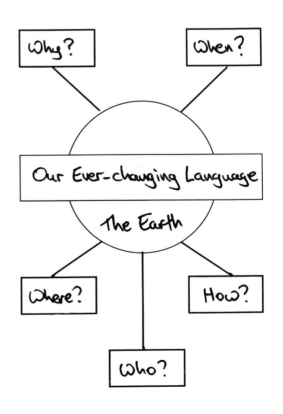

Plan 1 Clear, well-organised plan. Children would find suggested layout attractive and easy to follow. Concentrates on important issues in language change, each one highlighted by the box headings. Inter-connectedness of issues shown by repeated structural device of 'wh-' questions and logo. Central box announces subject of poster and serves as introduction to the topic. Layout would incline audience to read central box first. Writer has made material her own and guided audience through the topic. Good balance struck between information and examples.

Plan 2

a) Intro

b) History of lang   –   grammar
          vocab and meaning
          sounds

c) Conclusion

The next three plans were responses to this task:

Parklands, a registered nursery school for children between the ages of 2 and 5 years, is in the process of compiling an information pack for parents whose children are already enrolled, or who are about to enrol, at the nursery. This pack is intended to give parents an insight into day care and nursery education and also to give them confidence in *Parklands*.

You have been asked to contribute to the pack by writing the following sections:

Safety in the nursery
Play

You should provide information in an attractive and interesting way that aims to meet the needs of the intended audience.

You should write approximately 1100 words in total. The sections should be of roughly equal length.

Plan 3

2 sections – *safety in nursery* 550 words approx
              play 550 words approx
Audience = Parents (adults)
Safety in the nursery:
Persuasive – mention good points
Points to note:
   headings
   pictures
Sections for Safety
  i   Pride in Safety
  ii Notes – points at Parklands
  iii Equipment
  iv Complaints
  v Staff

Sections for Play:
  i   Diff ages
  ii Books and reading
  iii Lang and play
  iv Studies about children's play

Plan 4

2 sides of A4 for each section
  Safety ... Nursery
    Intro
  Who looks after children
    Picture of staff
  Authority list of factors
  Where
  Intro
  Play
  Intro

Plan 5

(Editor – I intend to produce my nursery pack in the form of large cards about 30 cm by 30 cm)
Plan
  Safety – general then specific
  Intro
a types of day care – the day care register
b must have fit persons and premises – our staff and premises
c meet local authority requirements – what are they; how we meet them
d key worker scheme
e safe toys; own transport
f parents at ease; feel free to come and have a look
  Play
a importance of play in child development
b what toys and games we have
c library
d play encourages talk and social skills
e equal opportunities
f timetable for typical day

ACTIVITY 17

This next exercise will give you an opportunity to practise your skills of organising and structuring material for a specific task.
Each of the following poems is written in a regional British dialect. Imagine that you have been commissioned to write the script for a short Radio 4 programme on 'Dialect Poetry'. The programme is to consist of a reading of these poems together with a script that both links the poems in some way and provides a context for them. You should thus ensure that your programme is a satisfactory whole and not just a series of disconnected readings. Write the script for this programme. You will need to:

- Try out a number of different ways in which the poems can be grouped or linked together.
- Choose what seems to be the best structure for the programme.
- Write the linking commentary.
- Write an introduction and conclusion to your programme.
- Write about 750 words, excluding the poems themselves.

You needn't concern yourself in this exercise with sound effects, music or any of the other conventions of a radio script. Remember that you should use *all* of the material provided.

TEXT 23

```
this is thi
six a clock
news thi
man said n
thireason
a talk wia
BBC accent
it coz yi
widny wahnt
mi ti talk
aboutthi
trooth wia
voice lik
wannayoo
scruff. if
a toktaboot
thitrooth
lik wanna yoo
scruff yi
widnythingk
it wuz troo.
```

```
jist wanna yoo
scruff tokn.
thirza right
way ti spell
ana right way
ti tok it. this
is me tokn yir
right way a
spellin. this
is ma trooth.
yoozdoantno
thitrooth
yirsellz cawz
yi canny talk
right. this is
the six a clock
nyooz. belt up.
```

Tom Leonard (Glasgow)

TEXT 24

```
'Ast ever swep a chimuck
Ta earn theeself a bob?
Old'Arry 'ave an' 'im da know
The'azards o' thic job
The neighbour's 'ad some soot down
The biggest pile 'er'd seen.
So 'er decides ta fetch a mon
Ta szwip thic blighter clean.
'Er goes across to 'Arry's
Ta ex 'im if'e knew
Of any mon wi' 'hout ta spare
Ta come an' szwip 'er flue.
Old 'Arry thought a minute
'Bout the merits of the job,
An' come ta the decision
That'e could use a bob.
"I'll szwip thee chimuck far tha"
Old 'Arry volunteered,
"Thou give I couple 'a 'ours
An' I'll 'ave thic blighter cleared"
Im shouted ta the neighbour
Ta take a look out back.
An' tell 'im when the brush wus through
Above the chimney stack
'Er stood outside about an hour
But nothing did appear.
Tho' 'Arry'd used up thirty rods
The top were no'where near.
```

K. Morgan (excerpt from *The 'Azards o' Chimuck Szwippin*)
(1978) (Gloucestershire)

TEXT 25

When ah were still nobbut a bairn

an were tekken along to t'schooil
t'teacher shewk'er'ead
med me feel a gurt fooil.
Shoe axed me wheear ah lived
an ah said, Oh just up t'rooad ...
Well, it's kinda 'omely like
is talkin' brooad.

Soa then she tewk me i' 'and
to learn me things, an by gosh
she sooin med me unnderstand
'at proper fowk talk posh.
It seeams they sa 'better' fer butter
an haitches you cannot afford
to drop – unless you're reight common
an talkin' brooad.

Soa ah sooin learned to put on an act
an talk wi a plum i' mi mahth,
when t'teacher were theear ah showed tact
an sahnded like sumbdy dahn sahth.
But as sooin as she'd gooan ah stopped
an dropt it just like a gurt luoad,
ah'd reyther, until ah get copt,
be talkin' brooad.

Kenneth Wadsworth (Talkin' Brooad) (1970s)
(Yorkshire)

TEXT 26

Last meal together, Leeds, the Queen's Hotel,
that grandish pile of swank in City Square.
Too posh for me! he said (though he dressed well)
If you weren't wi' me now ah'd nivver dare!

I knew that he'd decided that he'd die
not by the way he lingered in the bar,
nor by that look he'd give with one good eye,
nor the firmer handshake and the gruff *ta-ra,*
but when we browsed the station bookstall sales
he picked up *Poems from the Yorkshire Dales –*

*ere tek this un wi' yer to New York
to remind yer 'ow us gaffers used to talk.
It's up your street in't it? ah'll buy yer that!*

The broken lines go through me speeding South –
As t'Doctor stopped to oppen woodland yat ...
and
        wi' skill they putten wuds reet i' his mouth.
Tony Harrison (The Queen's English) (1981)
(Yorkshire)

TEXT 27

Eh, dear; there's bin some change in
Eawr heause this week or two;
Wheer once there used to be a din
It's like a Sunday schoo';
We never feight for apple pie,
We very seldom frap;

An' what d'ye think's the reason why?
Eawr Sarah's getten a chap.

Eawr fender shines just like a bell,
We'n had it silvered o'er;
An' th' cat appears to wesh itsel'
Moor often than before;
Eawr little Nathan's wiped his nose,
Eawr Jimmy's brushed his cap;
An' o this fuss is just becose
Eawr Sarah's getten a chap.
Sam Fitton (excerpt from Eawr Sarah's getten a chap) (c1900)
(Lancashire)

TEXT 28

Come carders an' spinners an' wayvers as
weel,
Stop yo'r frames an' yo'r jennies, strip roller
an' creel;
Let yo'r lathes cease to swing, an' yo'r
shuttles to fly,–
For there's gone through owd England a
leaud battle-cry,–
    Derry deawn!
They'n turned eaut at Ratchda' an' Owdham
an' Shay
An' th' Stalybridge lads are at Ash'n today;
'Fair wage for fair work' is the motto they'n
chose,
An' what'll be th' upshot no mortal man
knows.
    Derry deawn!

Eawr mesthers are screwin' eaur noses to th'
dust,
An' if we don't strike we'n no' maybe seen
th' wust;
They've cheeant up eaur bodies to slavery's
wheel,
And they'd sell, if we'd let 'em, eaur souls to
the diel.
    Derry deawn!
The Factory Worker's Song (1842) (Lancashire)

TEXT 29

Since I noo mwore do zee your feace
    Up stears or down below,
    I'll zit me in the lwonesome pleace,
    Where flat-bough'd beech do grow;
Below the beeches' bough, my love,
    Where you did never come,
An' I don't look to meet ye now,
    As I do look at hwome.

    Since you noo mwore be at my tide,
    In walks in zummer het,
I'll goo alwone where mist do ride,
    Drough trees a-drippen wet;

Below the rain-wet bough, my love,
  Where you did never come,
An' I don't grieve to miss ye now,
  As I do grieve at hwome.

William Barnes (excerpt from *The Wife a-lost*)
(1858) (Dorset)

TEXT 30

KIDSPOEM/BAIRNSANG
It wis January
and a gey dreich day
the first day I went to the school
so
ma Mum happed me up in ma good navyblue
  nap coat
wi the rid tartan hood
birled a scarf aroon ma neck
pu'ed on ma pixie and ma pawkies
it wis that bitter
said
'noo ye'll no starve'
gied me a wee kiss and a kidoan skelp on the bum
and sent me off across the playground
to the place I'd learn to say
'It was January
and a really dismal day
the first day I went to school
so
my Mother wrapped me up in my best navyblue
  top coat

with the red tartan hood
twirled a scarf around my neck
pulled on my bobble-hat and mittens
it was so bitterly cold
said
"now you won't freeze to death"
gave me a little kiss and a pretend slap on the
  bottom
and sent me off across the playground
to the place I'd learn to forget to say
"It wis January
and a gey dreich day
the first day I went to the school
so
ma Mum happed me up in ma good navyblue
  nap coat
wi the rid tartan hood
birled a scarf aroon ma neck
pu'ed on ma pixie and ma pawkies
it wis that bitter." '

Oh,
saying it was one thing
but when it came to writing it
in black and white
the way it had to be said
was as if
you were grown up, posh, male, English and
  dead.

Liz Lochhead (1970s)(Glasgow)

Introduction

You will probably think it odd to end this chapter with a section entitled 'Introduction'. In one sense, it is – introductions do come first in a text and the texts you write should be no exception. However, though introductions do come first, they ought not to be the first part of the text that you write. In fact, they could very well be the last. This isn't quite as crazy as it might sound; there are two main reasons. Firstly you need to be able to review the overall shape, structure and content of your completed text before you can introduce it properly and secondly, you will all know what can happen during the process of writing, even to the most meticulously planned piece. You can find yourself making changes as you write, because the very act of writing often sparks off new ideas either about the content or about the organisation of your text, however well you may have planned it. This doesn't mean, of course, that you need do no planning; the whole point of this chapter is to emphasise how important planning and structuring is. So the sensible advice must be to leave the writing of your introduction until the end. It *is* rather difficult to introduce something that hasn't yet been written.

One final note about introductions. They differ in kind from text type to text type. The introduction to a study pack will not be like the introduction to a talk, nor like the one to a newspaper article; some text types may forgo introductions entirely: a wall-poster, for example.

In this chapter you have learnt:

- that all texts need to be coherent if they are to be effective;
- that some text types have a 'given' structure, whilst others allow a writer freedom to decide on the structure for him or herself; and
- that it is vital that you plan the structure and organisation of your text before beginning to write.

Answer to Activity 14

The correct order for the paragraphs is: B F D C H A G E

4 Get Weaving

In Chapter 2 you saw that there were specific features and conventions associated with particular text types or genres and that you need to be familiar with as many of these genres as possible; in Chapter 3 you saw the importance of ensuring that any new text you write has a coherent shape and structure.

In this chapter, you are going to look at some of the ways of constructing your new text and weaving the parts of it together seamlessly.

You may have wondered why you have just read 'the ways of *constructing* your new text' rather than 'the ways of *writing* your new text'. You may also have noticed that on a number of occasions in the book the same or very similar expressions were used. After all, *writing* a text, whether in preparation for the examination or in the examination itself is what you do, isn't it? Well, up to a point, yes, that *is* what you are doing. But, as we have seen, any text that you write should be planned and organised, should have a shape. In that sense your text is an *artefact* or a *construct* – something made by human design or workmanship, or even, as we hope by craftsmanship. Think of yourself as a craftsman (or craftswoman) as you write, fashioning something that is entirely appropriate for its purpose.

The texts that you construct for this part of your examination course may be somewhat different from the ones that you produce in other parts, as these are made from source texts that have been provided for you, either in the assignment file or on the examination paper itself. What you are asked to do is to adapt these primary texts for their new audience. If we push the construction or building metaphor just a little further, these primary texts can be seen as the stones or bricks that will form your new building, but they will have to be shaped, altered or 'dressed' to fit in with its overall structure. Of course, not only do the stones or bricks have to be shaped to make them suitable, they have to be manoeuvred into position in accordance with the overall design or architecture. And, if we risk stretching the metaphor almost to breaking point, these building blocks need to be attached to each other with a variety of linking agents – mortar, bolts, welds and ties, for instance. It is these textual linking agents that form much of the subject matter of this chapter. We are going to examine how you can link the various parts of your text so that it forms a seamless whole. To steal the words of comedian Eric Morecambe about his long-suffering partner Ernie Wise's supposed wig, you should try to ensure that 'you can't see the join' in your new text.

The word *text* itself, as has been pointed out by an eminent linguist, is a metaphor. Its root lies in a Latin verb *texere*, meaning *to weave* and here is another apt image for the process upon which you are engaged. For this is exactly what you are doing when you produce a new text from your source material. You are weaving together threads from a variety of sources and creating something new. Just as a weaver uses many different threads to create her fabric, so you are using many different pieces of material to create your text. And just as you would think it poor craftsmanship if you were aware of any one of the separate pieces used to weave the fabric or any garment made from it (literally, 'if you could see the join'), so too must you ensure that your newly woven text appears seamless. The art lies in concealing the art.

So, in this chapter, we are going to examine some of those techniques that will enable you to do this. Some of them may appear slight, but they will still make a major contribution to your text construction and to the marks you will earn in the examination.

However, before we can do this, we should consider just how much of the original source material you ought to use in the construction of your new text. This is not quite as straightforward as it sounds, because different examination boards provide you with different amounts of material to read. Some can give you as many as 20–30 sides which may contain up to the same number of extracts, whilst others content themselves with four or five relatively short pieces. So most of the subsequent advice will concentrate on those boards that ask you to read and prepare a significant amount of material prior to the exam itself. This is sensible, because where you are dealing with only a relatively small amount of material which you see for the first time in the exam, then you will probably need to base your text on most, if not all, of it. So, let's assume that you have read and thoroughly prepared the material in an assignment file, as you were advised to do in Chapter 1. How much of it do you need to use? It's important at this point to clarify just what is meant by *use*.

Obviously you will not be able to include everything in your new text that is found in the assignment file, even if you rewrite it all, as this will mean you would exceed the word limit by a ludicrous amount; nor would you have the time to do so. You wouldn't have made any selection of material as the task requires. So the answer to the question is that you ought to extract material from *at least* 50% of the texts you have been given and have prepared. Let's put this in easy-to-understand figures. If, for example, your source file contained ten texts, then you should aim to use material from at least five of them as you weave your new script. This doesn't mean, of course, that you can't or shouldn't use material from any more than five source texts; indeed, many of the best scripts are woven using material from *all* of the sources provided; in this case, from all ten. What you should strenuously avoid is basing your text on material from only a small number of sources. The extreme in this case would be to use material from only one text, as this would hardly constitute weaving. If you use any fewer than four or five sources for your new text then remember you are seriously limiting your answer and thus limiting your chances of a good mark. Let's get clear, however, that you will *not* be using *everything* that is in each of your chosen source texts. You will need to select from them and decide how to use your selection. In fact, you may not be using very much from any one single source at all. One particular text may provide you with only one significant quotation, idea or illustration that you feel you should use.

So, you have now selected the material that you are going to use in the construction or weaving of your answer, having remembered to select from at least 50% of the sources, thus avoiding an excessively narrow or restricted range. What next?

Obviously, you begin to plan and compose your new text. This may well consist of a mixture of your own writing and material taken directly from the sources. You may decide that you want to cut some of this material out from the file and paste it into your new text, thus saving yourself the trouble of copying it out. This is a legitimate practice, but must be done with great care. It's very important to stress that cutting and pasting is NOT compulsory. You need *not* use the technique and indeed, many of the best answers in examinations are constructed without its aid. If, however, you decide to use cutting and pasting you must ensure:

- that you do not inadvertently exceed the word limit for the assignment;
- that the chosen extracts are integrated into your text;
- that your text does not contain too much of this cut-out material.

At the very most, any text that you compose should consist of no more than 40% of cut-out material. This should be the absolute maximum! If your script consists of more than this, you would be quite heavily penalised. Remember, you need not use any at all. To put this the other way round: your text must contain a minimum of 60% of your own new writing; many of the best scripts consist of nothing but the candidate's own new writing. But what exactly *is* 'new writing'?

Obviously, the nature of the new writing will vary from text to text, depending on its purpose and audience, but it can include:

- introductions
- conclusions or 'signings-off'
- links between sections of text
- summaries and paraphrases
- glosses, simplifications and explanations
- rewriting
- captions
- editorial features, such as headings and sub headings.

Some of these will be covered in the next chapter. This chapter, as you know, will concentrate on the ways you can ensure your text is woven together successfully, that it is *cohesive*. Don't forget, however, that the majority of any text you produce should consist of your own writing. Don't rely solely on the cut-and-paste method.

Keep those pronouns consistent

It can be at best frustrating and at worst confusing if a writer's use of pronouns is unclear. You should therefore ensure that yours is free from some of these more common faults:

- using pronouns without making clear who or what they refer to (the referent);
- using singular pronouns when the referent is plural (and vice-versa);
- altering the gender of the pronoun without the referent making the same change;
- failing to use pronouns where to do so would be stylistically more appropriate.

ACTIVITY 18

Here are five examples in which the writer has failed to use pronouns successfully. Identify the fault(s) and re-write the extracts to ensure that the meaning is clear. All are taken from the assignment in which candidates were asked to write the script for a talk to primary schoolchildren on caring for pet guinea pigs.

1   Who can tell me if I keep Maxi in a warm dry place and give her plenty of food and water all the time how many more years can Maxi live? (Answer) Another two years. Looking after Maxi is hard work. He needs attention all the time.

2   Remember that as well as playing with them you have to look after and care for them as well. If you want to buy a guinea pig go with your parent or another adult to a good pet shop where they will help you to pick a guinea pig which is healthy.

3   When you have bought your guinea pigs try and take it to a vet where it can have a check up, and where you can take it if it ever looks ill.

4   Guinea pigs are suitable for first time pets. They can be easy and cheap to keep. But guinea pigs should be looked after properly. Guinea pigs are easy-going, clean and friendly. Guinea pigs are sometimes seen as boring but they are not.

5   It is very important that a guinea pig has a healthy balanced diet. They also have to have vitamins. They get Vitamin B from eating their own droppings. Vitamin C is essential for them as it helps them to get rid of acids in their tummy's. Vitamin C can be bought and added to their water. Guinea pigs should be given fresh food and water every day.

Don't get your syntax in a twist

You'll have been told time and time again by your teachers that you should always check your work carefully before handing it in. They are right! The same advice is repeated here. If the writers of the next examples had bothered to follow this advice, then they probably wouldn't have produced such convoluted sentence structures as these which are very difficult for the reader to disentangle and make sense of. When you are writing in a pressure situation, such as an exam, some *minor* errors are bound to creep into your work and allowance is made for this. If, however, poor syntax impedes comprehension then questions are asked by examiners about the writer's ability to practise his or her craft successfully.

ACTIVITY 19

The following examples are all taken from the assignment referred to on pp 18–19 in which candidates had to write a tape-script guiding visitors round an exhibition of Rodin's sculptures. Re-write them so that the meaning becomes crystal clear. Remember they are meant to be listened to.

1 The first statue titled 'The Thinker' which was originally called 'The Poet' until he changed the title due to him widening the theme he had originally come up with, so that it would become more universal, was the work on which Rodin concentrated all his best energies ...

2 The battle over 'The Age of Bronze' helped focus public attention all the more on the talents of the man who involuntarily provoked it and paved the way for the object of public scandal in sculpting in which he was to become the acknowledged master.

3 Rodin's aim was accomplished for as we enter Room One of the exhibit, you can see his premiere piece 'The Age of Bronze'. This is known to be Rodin's first real showpiece exhibited in Brussels during the winter of 1877. It is the piece responsible for catapulting him to fame due to the controversy with which it was received by the public.

The mystery of anaphoric, cataphoric and exophoric reference

This is less fearsome than the title might lead you to believe and such reference usually occurs through use of pronouns.

Anaphoric reference points the reader back to something mentioned earlier in a text; for example, 'The man was last seen eating a bag of fish and chips outside a cafe in Huddersfield. He was wearing a black denim jacket.' *He* is anaphoric because it refers back to *the man*.

Cataphoric reference points the reader forward to something that will occur later in the text. For example, in the next sentence *these* is cataphoric because it points forward to *the measures*: 'These are the measures we shall take'.

In the main, anaphora and cataphora cause little problem to writers and readers, but as always you must be on the alert to ensure that your use of pronouns is clear. However, you should try to avoid *exophoric* reference. This occurs when a writer refers to something outside the text s/he is writing and usually causes puzzlement to a reader or listener. For example, this extract from the Rodin assignment contains exophoric references:

The Societé des Gens des Lettres had wanted a statue of Balzac to be placed on a site in Paris. The work had been originally entrusted to Chapu in 1888 but sadly he died in 1891, leaving only the beginning of his work. At the suggestion of some of his friends, Rodin wrote to the Societé offering to do the work and the offer was accepted.

Because the writer had made no previous reference to *Balzac, Chapu* or *The Societé des Gens des Lettres,* the listener would be wondering about their identity or significance.

Make those transitions smooth

It can sometimes be very disconcerting for a reader or listener if a writer or speaker suddenly jumps from one topic to the next without first having signalled that this is about to happen. It's rather like going on a train driven by an inexperienced driver, who doesn't quite know how to brake or start off smoothly. The journey seems to proceed in fits and starts and, as a result, passengers are unable to relax and enjoy the ride because they aren't quite sure that the recently purchased cups of coffee aren't about to spill painfully into their laps. Readers and passengers alike require a smooth journey. As a writer, therefore, you should ensure that the journey through your text is as pleasant as possible for your readers. To illustrate a jerky journey through a text consider this next extract from the guinea pig assignment.

When I have finished talking I will be happy to answer any questions you may have. To find out what sex your guinea pig is, hold it carefully when it is lying on its back and gently press the lower part of its tummy. Guinea pigs are very easy to handle, they don't bite very often and are easy to hold because they don't fidget. Guinea pigs are not too big, they grow to about the length of the 30 cm rulers you use at school . . .

The writer of this passage doesn't signal her changes of topic very well. Having indicated that she is willing to answer questions, she launches directly into the inappropriately chosen topic of sexing guinea pigs without any preliminary introduction. Then she makes an abrupt transition to handling them and another to their size. It would have been a comparatively simple matter for her to have signalled her transitions by remarks such as *Now, I'm going to begin by telling you how to find out if your pet is a boy or girl guinea pig. This is very important* or *Let's now turn to.*

There are many such signalling devices available to writers which can help readers on a journey through a text. These can range from the formal such as *There are four stages in this process: the first is . . .* or *As a result . . .* to the more informal such as *Moving swiftly on, we can see . . .* or *So, then . . .* Naturally, different text types will have different signalling devices and they will also vary depending on the purpose of the text and the nature of the audience. One of the best ways that you can prepare for the construction of your new text is to study the methods that other writers use in various text types. Your work on stylistics will be of great value here.

ACTIVITY 20

The following passage is the opening of a student's answer to the guinea pig assignment. Re-write it so that it is wholly suited to its audience and task. Obviously, you'll need to pay attention to the transitions, but you will also need to re-write sections that sound more like the written than the spoken word. Decide whether the way that the student has begun the talk is likely to appeal to young primary school children.

TEXT 31

Guinea pigs in the wild needed to be able to survive. Because of their small size many larger animals would eat them so it was necessary for them to know the area they lived in well. They communicate with each other all the time by making different sounded squeaks. How many of you have a guinea pig? Do you do as much as you can for it? It is best to feed and clean your guinea pig so that it is healthy and happy. In fact, do you know that you can train your guinea pig to do tricks like you would a dog. Take three bowls. One red, one blue and one yellow. Only fill one of these bowls with food and leave the others empty. Let the hungry guinea pig run from one end of the room towards the bowls. When it knows which bowl contains the food move the bowl to another place and let it find it again. A pet guinea pig isn't all fun, you do need to do a lot of work because, although you don't need to walk a guinea pig every day like you would a dog you do need to clean its hutch out every day because guinea pigs need to go to the toilet just like us, but they can't flush the toilet afterwards.

Make your extractions painless!

There may be occasions when you want to incorporate extracts from the original source material into your new text. You may, for instance, want to use an appropriate quotation from an expert or you may need to use information from official sources. Whatever the reason, if you do use short extracts, then there are a number of pitfalls it is best to avoid. These come under two main headings.

1 When you weave the extract into your own writing, you should make sure that it is grammatically, syntactically and stylistically cohesive. To do this you might therefore have to change the tenses or the pronouns of the extract to fit in with the approach you have chosen and, of course, you will need to make sure that the syntactic links between what you write and what is written in the extract are smooth.

2 When you want to use an extract without altering its words, you should ensure that you provide a context for it. This will prevent any confusion on the part of the reader or listener if just before the extract you write for instance:

   In 1945, Prime Minister Winston Churchill said in the House of Commons …
   or
   the great art critic Herbert Read wrote of Rodin's sculpture …
   or
   Official statistics from the 1991 Census show that …

Each of these brief examples gives sufficient information to enable the readers or listeners to put the extracts you are about to use into their proper contexts and prevent them being puzzled by the vast difference in style between your words and Churchill's!

ACTIVITY 21

Here are three short passages from one student's answer to the Rodin assignment. Remember the task was to write a tape script guiding visitors around the Museum. In each of the passages, the student has included material directly from the sources, but as you will see, has not really incorporated them successfully. There are major stylistic clashes between what she writes and the original source. Imagine you were her editor and that you had to re-write the passages in such a way that there was no clash of styles.

TEXT 32

Let's move on now to the second sculpture marked on your plan. This is one of Rodin's most famous pieces and it's called *The Walking Man*. You'll easily be able to see why. Rodin completed this vigorous work in 1877. It lacks the old values of identity, assertive ego, completeness of parts and of finish, but more than any other of Rodin's works, this sculpture is meant to overwhelm us by the power of movement. Look carefully and you'll see that Rodin achieved his aim.

TEXT 33

In front of you you can see the piece known as *The Age of Bronze*. This sculpture retains a freshness and an authority that depends on its containment of structure and understatement of handling. Rodin at the time was accused of making a sketch rather than a finished sculpture. At the time when it was first

exhibited it was accused of being too lifelike. Unfortunately for Rodin, these accusations spread to France and they were eagerly circulated by a number of not so well meaning sculptors.

TEXT 34

We now arrive at *The Prodigal Son*. I like this. He seems to be reaching to God looking for help. Paul, information please.

Paul (reading)   56–57. THE PRODIGAL SON. Before 1889. Bronze.

$54\frac{3}{4} \times 41\frac{1}{2} \times 27\frac{3}{4}$

This work, which figures in the right hand folding door of *The Gate*, was probably conceived between 1885 and 1887, for the subject is used in the *Fugit Amor*, which is prior to 1887.

ACTIVITY 22

Sometimes it's possible to let quotations 'speak' for themselves because the context of your own writing makes it clear who is speaking. On other occasions, you'll need to ascribe words to the speaker. In doing this lots of student writers overuse 'said' (or sometimes 'stated'). If every time you use a quotation you introduce it by *Raymond Wagstaff said . . . Teddy Rabbett said. . . Beatrice Smallweed said . . .* ad infinitum, the result is that your writing becomes tedious and predictable. You should aim to vary the words and the ways in which words are ascribed to someone else. Here are a few suggestions:

remarked / in the words of / expressed his views thus / asserted / observed

Collect as many more of these as you can. Bring in a variety of texts to class and see how many ways you can find that this is done. If you look in a thesaurus you should also find plenty of ideas.

Make your captions count

There may be times when you want to use illustrations and photographs as part of your new text. These might either be ones that have been included in the source material or on the examination paper itself. Indeed you might feel that your new text would be enhanced by illustrations that you yourself suggest to the editor. In this latter case, you need not draw these illustrations, merely give a brief written outline of your requirements (or a quick sketch, if you wish). The important factor in your use of illustrations is that you provide appropriate captions for them. Readers of your text would find it very frustrating if you had included an illustration or photograph and they were left wondering just what was its significance or indeed exactly <u>what</u> it was. So, in most circumstances, you should include a brief caption. There are a number of ways you can do this:

- use the one that was originally provided in the source material. This might not always be suitable because of its style or level of difficulty and you thus need to be wary of taking over such captions wholesale;
- compose a caption of your own that is appropriate for the audience and purpose of your text;
- make a reference to the illustration in the body of your text by writing something such as *in Figure 1, you can see . . .* In this case you must ensure that you clearly label what is meant to be Figure 1 in your text.

The most important thing to remember is that any illustrations you include should be an integral part of your text. The golden rule in the use of illustrations is: if they don't contribute to or enhance the meaning of your text, don't use them. Remember that you are trying to demonstrate your skills as a writer, not as an illustrator or graphic designer. This means that there should be no place in your text for such things as, for example:

- borders of daffodils surrounding texts on Wordsworth;
- 19th century black and white pictures of lead miners that have been carefully coloured in;
- pseudo-Chinese writing dividing the sections of a text on recent events in that country;
- drawings of bagpipers and caber-tossers adorning the text of a report on the tourist potential of the Western Scottish islands.

These are all real examples that contributed nothing to the meaning of the texts and, no doubt, wasted a lot of the writer's time. Sensible use of illustrations for these same assignments included:

- a captioned picture of Wordsworth's cottage in the Lakes where he composed some of his most famous poems;
- labelled maps of the 19th century lead mining areas in the North East of England;
- pictures of the Chinese leaders who ordered the massacre at Tiananmen Square in 1989;
- a bar chart illustrating the growth in the number of visitors to the Western Isles between 1960 and 1990.

Other communication strategies

The example above of the bar chart should serve to remind you that there are other ways of communicating than writing continuous prose and that you should consider using some of these, where appropriate, in your new text. We've already looked at some of these in the book, but here are a few more suggestions:

bar charts   fact boxes   question and answer   time lines   texts within texts.

1 In pairs, or small groups, collect a range of different types of publication (books, magazines, leaflets, posters, for example).
2 List all the different communication strategies used by the writers in these publications.

3 Write a short guide advising A-Level English Language students about the range of strategies open to them in their writing and illustrating each strategy's effectiveness.

The art of summary

A key skill that you need to practise is that of summary and paraphrase. We've already briefly looked at this in the first chapter when we were considering how best you can prepare for the examination as you read the source material. It's also a skill you will probably need to use in the construction of your new text, as you do have to re-present some of the original material in your own words. We've seen the dangers of over-reliance on using extracts verbatim – you run the risk of stylistic and syntactic clashes and of over-shooting any prescribed word limit. So, summarising should be an important part of your armoury. Unfortunately, it can be all too easy to make bad summaries. We've all probably had the experience of being pinned in a corner and forced to listen whilst a friend tells us about the great film she saw last night; she relates all the twists and turns of an intricate plot, only to backtrack because she's just remembered some indispensable piece of information. The end result is highly confused – and so are you.

Again, you've probably had to borrow someone else's notes because you've missed a class only to find that the notes are impossible to follow because whilst your friend has written out in full detail the teacher's illustrations of his general argument, he's missed the essential points. All you are left with is a collection of disconnected jottings, because there is no clear thread running through the summary.

A good summary, then, must retain the essential points of the original, present these points in a clear logical manner and, of course, use language that is entirely appropriate for the task in hand. There are four basic skills involved in making a summary:

■ substituting general or generic terms for specific detail and particular examples
■ eliminating unnecessary words and expressions
■ locating the central topic(s) in a paragraph
■ paraphrasing these essential points.

The use of generic terms

One very simple method of 'losing' words is to substitute a generic term (a word that applies to a whole class or group) for a number of related items. For example, you could replace the underlined words in this extract from an estate agent's brochure by the one word *property*:

Consult our brochure if you want the best selection of *houses*, *cottages*, *flats*, *bungalows* and *rented accommodation* in the area.

ACTIVITY 24

Choose a suitable generic term for the underlined items in these next sentences.

1 Inflation affects the standard of living of not only the <u>doctor</u>, the <u>solicitor</u> and <u>chartered accountant</u> but also of the <u>garage mechanic, the refuse collector and the plumber.</u>
2 Before he went on holiday, he went to the newsagent to cancel his regular order for <u>The Guardian, Sunday Times, The Times Educational Supplement, Private Eye and Men's Fitness.</u>
3 Before the members of the visiting team left the dressing room, <u>their money, wrist watches and anything else that might attract the attention of a thief</u> were locked away <u>in order to facilitate the avoidance of the possibility of theft.</u>

Eliminating unnecessary words

You probably noticed that the last example was different than the first two. You didn't need to use a generic word for *in order to facilitate the avoidance of the possibility*; 'to prevent' would have done just as well, because it's much more direct and succinct.

ACTIVITY 25

The following passage is an extreme example of circumlocution (indirect long-windedness) and jargon. Identify the unnecessary words and expressions and then rewrite the whole passage so that its essence is expressed in the shortest possible number of words.

TEXT 35

When he was approached on the subject of whether there was any possible course of action he could adopt in order to check the rise in unemployment, the President replied that at this moment in time he saw no other option but to reply in the negative. While he was freely prepared to concede that the continually recurrent problem of unemployment was, of course, in his opinion one of the gravest and most serious problems faced by the Western world and one which threatened every single citizen and individual because of its destructive effect on the future ahead, he felt nevertheless that in fact the remedial solution to the problem did not lie within the Administration's effectual parameters of ameliorative decision making.

Locating the essential points

When you are looking for the essential points in a passage, you will often find that a well-constructed paragraph is built around one or two central topics. Your summary will then involve a process of separating this central topic from its surrounding amplifications and supporting examples.

ACTIVITY 26

Read the following paragraph and then using a sentence of around 20 of your own words, write down what you consider to be its central idea. Do this before reading on.

TEXT 36

After years of predictions about its importance in industry, commerce, education and the home, information technology now affects most of us in some way. Several industries are being transformed by robot assembly techniques; commerce is increasingly reliant on electronic storage and transmission of information; many schools and colleges routinely teach computing as part of the general curriculum; home shopping and banking have arrived. Medicine, cinema, policing, transport, law; the penetration is wide. Skills too are affected; managers are increasingly expected to master information-management tools like database and financial planning packages; large numbers of teachers must at least understand the elements of computer technology; word-processing skills are demanded of office workers, and many factory workers must come to grips with computerised machine-tools, which change the pattern of their work and reduce the value of traditional manual skills in favour of mental ones.

COMMENTARY

This is what one student wrote in answer to the question:

Most people's lives have been changed by information technology, after years of predictions about its importance.

This is a fair summary, as the central topic of the paragraph is introduced in the first sentence and the remainder of the passage consists of a string of examples that illustrate the writer's general point. However, you'll have noticed that the student actually used a whole phrase from the original passage in her summary: *after years of predictions about its importance*. So, whilst the student's summary does contain the essential point of the passage, it may not be appropriate, because it is a direct quotation.

You may need to summarise using words which are not direct quotations because of the audience and purpose of your new text. You should always keep in mind who you are writing for and why you are writing. This, you will remember, is the key to success in this part of your English Language course. Your choice of language must always be appropriate to the task, even when you are summarising. So, be wary about using direct quotation in summaries.

In this chapter you have learnt about the techniques involved in constructing a new text and how to integrate material from your sources successfully into the body of this new text.

5 Finding the Right Voice

Now, boys and girls, we're going to look at something really exciting in this chapter. I'm sure you're going to enjoy it. We're going to be looking at 'voice'. That's right, 'voice'. It won't be too difficult, so I want you to try really hard with this super new topic so that you can all have a lot of fun learning new things and, at the same time, get really good marks for your work. That's great, isn't it? So, are you all ready? Then let's begin! Off we go!

Tone of voice

Let's start again! We certainly need to because if the chapter continued in this manner or, heaven forbid, the whole book were written like this, then it's a fair assumption that you would cease to take it seriously and would consign it to the back of your locker where it would lie gathering dust. And deservedly so. Why? Because the book would not be addressing you in a manner suitable for what we presume is the majority of its audience – 17 and 18 year old A-Level students of English Language. You may, of course, think that the book doesn't speak to you very effectively anyway, but that isn't on account of the writer not trying to do so. In fact, the tone used at the start of this chapter would almost certainly be a turn-off for *any* audience. Those of you who are familiar with the dramatic monologue of the comedian, Joyce Grenfell, in which she parodies the efforts of a well-meaning but ineffectual primary school teacher to gain the attention of her pupils may well recognise something of the flavour of the opening paragraph. In fact, were this chapter part of an A-Level English Language assignment, then the writer/candidate would certainly have failed the examination. You will remember that the first question an examiner asks about a candidate's work is whether it would be effective in achieving its purpose. In this case, it certainly would not be.

The reason for this lack of effectiveness is, of course, the tone of voice chosen by the writer to address his readers. Any reader would soon cease his reading if addressed in such a manner. 'Voice', then is an extremely important factor in the success or failure of your writing and indeed, all examiners pay close attention to it.

So far in this chapter we have made little distinction between *speaking* and *writing*. For instance in *you may, of course, think that the book doesn't speak very effectively to you anyway but that isn't on account of the writer not trying to do so* you find that the book is *speaking* whilst at the same time having a *writer*. In fact, we use the expression *tone of voice* to refer both to speech and to writing. We can be offended by or persuaded by the tone adopted by a speaker just as much as one adopted by a writer. In both cases, one individual (writer or speaker) is addressing another individual (reader or listener).

To address someone involves tone. It's impossible to address someone without doing so. So to overcome any potential confusion, the terms *addresser* (the person doing the addressing) and *addressee* (the person being addressed) are sometimes used. There are of course, an enormous number of tones available to both speakers and writers: you can be wheedling, hectoring, friendly, brusque, comic, authoritative, hesitant and so on. It's just a matter of choosing the appropriate tone of voice to achieve your purpose.

A human voice is individual; your personality is reflected in your voice. It might be affected by many other factors such as your age, gender, socio-economic status and regional origin, but not everyone of your age, gender, socio-economic status and regional origin has a voice like yours. Your voice *is* you. Think how often we can recognise people by their voice alone, even on the telephone or consider how often we rush to judge someone solely on the basis of his or her voice. So it's clearly very important to choose the appropriate voice for your writing. The same one will not be suitable for every audience and every purpose. One of the worst mistakes you can make is always to write in the same flat 'voiceless' tone for every audience. The individuality of the speaker or writer should come through in most text-types, though there are some in which it is better that individuality or personality is absent. It would be inappropriate, for instance, if there were a strong personal voice in the report of an inquiry into a rail accident or in an employment contract. This doesn't, of course, mean that such texts should not be clearly written and easy to understand. Particular text-types will demand particular types of voice.

ACTIVITY 27

The following passages have all been chosen because there is a clear voice in each one. Read them carefully and then:

1 write a short profile or character sketch, of not more than 50 words, of the addresser constructed by each text. In other words, what kind of person appears to be addressing the reader?
2 list the ways, together with supporting evidence from the text in which the writer has used language to construct this addresser. You might need to consider lexis, grammatical structures and levels of formality, for example.

TEXT 37

Are you sitting comfortably?

Good. Then, welcome to the first issue of *Sofastyle*.

It's a magazine designed to be of interest regardless of whether you are about to invest in a new sofa or not.

But if you are, we hope our magazine will give you plenty of useful advice in helping you to make the perfect choice for your home.

We have consulted the experts to find out what you should look out for, which styles and colours are likely to suit you personally and how to care for your sofa once you've bought it. We also talked to the stars about the secret sofa lifestyles of the rich and famous, and there are some great money saving offers too.

It all adds up to an exciting lifestyle magazine no sofa shopper should be without.

So just sit back and enjoy it.

Sarah Barton

Editor

TEXT 38

Use your time wisely

Employers, when considering graduate applications, look for evidence of skills, aptitudes and personal qualities to meet particular criteria. These could include, for example: team skills; good written and verbal communication; motivation; ability to work under pressure; analytical and problem solving skills; leadership; enthusiasm and interpersonal skills.

Of course, you will hopefully have developed some of these through your academic courses and outside interests and activities. However, if you use your vacations wisely, it will help ensure that your future applications will be more attractive to employers.

Never mind developing skills, I need to pay off my overdraft/ finance my inter-rail trip!

Fair enough – these are valid reasons for taking a particular job. However, all experience has its value. For example you may decide to take a job working long shifts, packing in a factory because it pays well. Even though this will not stretch you intellectually and you may find it very boring or physically draining, it will have taught you, for example, to work with others and to work under pressure. Bar work and shop work similarly will teach you how to deal with customers

and possibly have responsibility for supervising others or handling money.

TEXT 39

In this unit, you have developed your knowledge of stories and storytelling. You have also learned skills in oral and written storytelling. You may wish to build on these experiences by doing some further activities:

- Start a storytelling group in your class or school, but do not make the group too large. Agree to meet regularly to swap ideas and tell stories.
- Try to listen to as many storytellers in performance as possible. You may be able to ask them about their experiences as a storyteller.
- Talk to friends and relatives and ask them if they know any stories to tell you. Ask them if you can tape record them telling their stories. Your relatives will be able to remember stories from before you were born. You could write these down and make your own anthology.

TEXT 40

If you're a HOT FIRE ARIES, you're an independent soul and you throw yourself into everything you do 100 per cent. If you ever have any boy-related problems, you'd do well to listen to a few words of wisdom from those who really care about you.

If you're a HOT FIRE LEO you are very good at getting your own way, especially in romance. Once you decide what, or who, you really, really want there's no stopping you!

If you're a HOT FIRE SAGITTARIUS you are one crazy chick and you've been known to eat boys for breakfast! But you've got a deep and sensitive side too, which you don't mind showing off to the right boy.

Some very skilful writers deliberately choose an inappropriate voice, usually for comic or satiric purposes. The humour stems from the incongruous contrast between the voice and the content. For instance, in this short extract from Jonathan Swift's 'A Modest Proposal' (1729) the voice the writer chooses is that of an eminently reasonable man who proposes an eminently unreasonable solution for the hardship inflicted on the Irish by the English. He proposes that children should be bred, like cattle, for the table.

TEXT 41

I do therefore humbly offer it to public consideration, that of the hundred and twenty thousand children, already computed, twenty thousand may be reserved for breed, whereof only one fourth part to be males, which is more than we allow to sheep, black-cattle, or swine, and my reason is that these children are seldom the fruits of marriage, a circumstance not much regarded by our savages, therefore one male will be sufficient to serve four females. That the remaining hundred thousand may at a year old be offered in sale to the persons of quality, and fortune, through the kingdom, always advising the mother to let them suck plentifully in the last month so as to render them plump, and fat for a good table.

Not all discrepancies between voice and content have such an overtly political purpose as Swift's, of course. Many writers enjoy the comic effect alone.

ACTIVITY 28

So far you have read different voices on different subjects. In this next activity there are three different voices on the same subject, the pioneer jazz pianist and band leader, Jelly Roll Morton.

1 Read each passage carefully and discuss, in pairs, the following questions:
  a What assumptions can be made about the intended readership of each text?
  b What tones of voice are being used to address the reader?
  c What are the distinctive features of the language of each passage?
2 Based solely on the information in these texts, write a two hundred word script for a Radio 2 continuity announcer that informs listeners about a 30 minute programme of Jelly Roll Morton's music to be broadcast later in the week. The script should also tempt people to listen to the programme. Of course, you'll need to establish the appropriate voice for your script.

TEXT 42

The grooviest sounds in jazz aren't always the latest, you know! Grab hold of the recordings of Jelly Roll Morton – dig that name, better not ask where it came from!! – and you'll be back in the brothels and dance halls of the Big Easy where jazz first saw the light of day. Or night, I should say! J R really wanted to be the world's greatest pool player, but pool's loss was jazz's gain as you'll soon tell when you listen to that ol' joanna. Catch his mould-breaking mix of ragtime, blues and minstrel songs and you'll think yourself sippin' whiskey and munchin' on a po' boy down on Bourbon Street right there in the heart of New Orleans.

TEXT 43

JELLY ROLL MORTON claimed jazz was his invention. It wasn't, but he invented or enhanced enough of its components to make the claim forgivable. In helping ragtime swing, and liberating the improviser, he was a towering figure of proto-jazz. Ragtime was his primary influence, but not as played by ragtime piano gurus. Morton improvised, and his interpretation of ragtime did not pursue the ideals of a stately formal black music like Joplin's: it took a more spontaneous, unruly form. He upset ragtime's regular metres and expanded the instrumentation of the orthodox New Orleans band to feature groups of instruments playing harmonically, as in the Red Hot Peppers' 'clarinet sections'.

TEXT 44

Morton was the first important jazz composer. His compositions, many written long before he began recording, represent a rich synthesis of Afro-American musical elements, particularly as embodied in the pure New Orleans collective style which he helped to develop to its finest expression. Paradoxically, his emphasis on composition and well-rehearsed, co-ordinated performances was unique and antithetical to the primarily extemporised, polyphonic New Orleans style. In his best ensemble work, especially with the Red Hot Peppers, Morton showed that composition and meticulously rehearsed arrangements were not incompatible with the spontaneity of improvised jazz but could in fact retain and enhance it. In this respect Morton's achievement may be ranked with that of

Duke Ellington, Thelonious Monk, Charles Mingus, and Gil Evans.

Morton's sophisticated conception of jazz is all the more remarkable since the origins of his style lie primarily in classic midwestern ragtime and simple instrumental blues. His piano pieces (such as *Grandpa's Spells* and *Kansas City Stomp*) strongly resemble ragtime in their form, but by elaborating these works with composed and improvised variation Morton was able to transcend ragtime's formal conventions. Ultimately he freed ragtime from its narrow strictures by developing within it an ensemble style embracing homophony, improvised polyphony, solo improvisations, breaks, and a constant variation of texture and timbre.

A note on register and style

You'll have noticed that although the three texts about Jelly Roll Morton were more or less written on the same subject – his musicianship – they were distinctly different in style. They quite neatly illustrate the difference between two terms which are sometimes confused: register and style. The three pieces, not surprisingly, all used lexis from the world of music – *ragtime, blues, composition, arrangement, improvisation* and so on. This then is the *register* of the passages: a set of words all concerned with the same subject, in this case, music. But, though the register remains the same, it would be difficult to confuse the styles in which Texts 42 and 44 were written. The two styles differ because the passages were written for totally different audiences, neither of whom would dream of reading the other. It would, however, be possible for them to have been written by the same skilful author (they weren't!) who had a repertoire of styles and carefully varied them to suit each audience. Indeed, this is exactly what you are asked to do in this part of your A-Level course: to choose a style of writing or voice to suit a particular audience and purpose.

Register is a set of lexical items that are all on the same subject; style, a set of distinctive linguistic features that a writer has selected in order to write about the subject for a particular audience. An analogy from the world of clothes might make this distinction clear. There are some occasions when it is expected that men will wear a suit – job interviews and formal dinners are two of these. There are other occasions, however, when both men (and women) could wear a T-shirt and jeans. We could say that the 'register' of some occasions is a suit and of others, a T-shirt and jeans. But there are many possible variations of style within the 'suit register' – single-breasted or double breasted, for example. Similarly there are variations of style possible within the 'jeans register': straight, bootleg and hipster, for instance. Texts can be viewed in the same way. There are recognised and appropriate registers for all football reports or all film reviews, but there are variations within these registers that allow the reader to see that a football report or film review for one magazine or newspaper can differ in style from one written for another.

Now that you have not only a clear idea of what 'voice' is but also how important it is for you to write in an appropriate one, let's have a look at what some students wrote in response to one particular assignment. Here's what they were asked to do. The material they were asked to work with was a set of extracts about Killhope Wheel Lead Mining Centre in County Durham, the best preserved lead mining site in Britain. Their assignment was to write the text for an educational pack for use with secondary school GCSE pupils aged 14–16 which was designed to prepare the pupils for and interest them in their forthcoming visit to the centre. So you can see that this was a very challenging audience for which to write. Get the voice wrong and the pupils would be very quickly turned off from the whole idea of visiting Killhope or from having any interest whatsoever in lead-mining. The writer needs to work hard to interest them in this particular subject, anyway. Imagine your response to a school textbook or educational pack that failed to speak to you interestingly. After all, the audience for this assignment would have been *you* only one or two years ago! So it was vital for these writers to choose an appropriate voice. Let's see if they managed it.

ACTIVITY 29

There are five short extracts from students' work, each one taken from the beginning of the assignment. There is a brief commentary on the first one, but the others are provided without comment. You should discuss these in pairs and:

1 write a detailed commentary on each one, paying particular attention to the voice adopted by the writer. The important question to ask is whether you think it would succeed in attracting the attention and interest of the reader;

2 rewrite any passage that you think would have been unsuccessful;

3 place the five passages in a rank order, beginning with the one that you think would best stimulate the pupils into wanting to visit Killhope and ending with the one that would turn them off social and economic history for ever!

TEXT 45

Work in the lead mines

Lead from other countries forced the price of British lead down and by 1896 the British lead industry had collapsed. We can see this from the prices shown below which show the price per ton.

1865	£21.05	1880	£17.41
1874	£22.63	1881	£15.72
1875	£23.17	1882	£15.45
1876	£22.55	1883	£14.07
1877	£21.49	1884	£12.58
1878	£18.74	1885	£12.25
1879	£15.42		

Despite this Killhope Wheel has remained intact and so you may come and visit this centre and be transported back in time, to a different era and a different culture! (Or you can look at it from a 20th century point of view. It makes no difference to us).

Often boys your age and younger would be working in the mines! Some would even be ten years old! They were mainly 'washers'. From one boy's point of view this meant:

'When I first went to washing I turned the handle of the thing in which they wash the stuff, the buddle. I next went to drawing slime. There is a trunk and water comes over it, and a boy puts in the slime, and we rub it with a colrake, and the water runs through it, and washes away all the mud, and leaves the lead.'

This was *not* thought of as hard work, compared to the coal mines.

TEXT 46

An introduction to the Killhope Lead Mining Centre

The words 'lead mining' may cause you to groan inwardly and think 'Oh no how boring'. This information pack has been designed especially for 14–16 year olds to prove otherwise. This pack will give you a detailed and hopefully interesting insight to the Killhope lead mines and visitors' centre based in the North Pennine Ore field.

Due to cheaper sales of lead from Australia, Mexico and the US, it is not mined in common practise today. The industry blossomed in the 17 and 18 hundreds. Lead is found in veins in the form of lead bearing ore. These usually descend to great depths but because the lead quality gets poorer the deeper it is most mines were less than 600ft deep. Most veins were 2 or 3 foot wide so could be mined from above + below simultaneously. Wooden levels could be inserted on a timber framework to give access to various work faces.

TEXT 47

Killhope Wheel Lead Mining Centre

Over 200 years ago, lead was found at Killhope, it was like a gold rush. New people moved into the area to find work, shafts were being built and soon enough the lead mining industry took over the North of England.

No lead is mined today in Northumberland. For almost a century the mines and smelt mills have been silent apart from the reworking of old levels and spoil heaps for flourite and barite.

But now, Killhope Wheel is turning again and we are open to the public. Come and see how lead was extracted and how miners lived all those years ago. It's a great experience and educational too.

In this pack we have put together some pieces of information that will enhance your visit to Killhope Wheel.

TEXT 48

Home on Killhope Common

Northumbrian lead mining – it doesn't sound very interesting, does it? But for the miners and families of Killhope, lead meant everything. Thanks to their hard work last century, this century we can explore the areas where they worked and make valuable discoveries, besides having fun seeing friends disappear into the darkness as they walk down the underground network!

Why Killhope?

Today, Killhope Wheel Lead Mining centre doesn't actually produce any lead, but when lead was discovered upstream in 1853 a new mine was started to reach the 'lead veins' which would then be excavated. By the mid 1870s the mine had become rich. A company – W B Lead – built the wheel which stands proud today, besides the surrounding buildings and a new plant started production in 1878. What you will see on your visit to Killhope are the buildings of that time, the Park Level Mine.

TEXT 49

If your family lived in Killhope in 1878 the chances are that they would all be involved in the lead mining industry, as would most other people you knew.

Your father would work in a team or partnership with 3 or 4 other men. Their job would be to extract lead from the veins underground with either gunpowder or a pick.

Your mother would possibly not work at the lead mines as many women stayed at home looking after their house and their plot of land.

You would probably work on the ore-dressing floors and work underground during the three winter months when ore-dressing was not in operation. You would be a labourer for a mining partnership. Today this would be called an apprenticeship.

COMMENTARY The opening to Text 45 is a mixed bag. It begins very dully, with the table of figures in particular being very likely to put the 14 year old reader off. The voice chosen is that of the textbook writer and there is no attempt to engage with the audience. A bad start! Then the writer seems to realise her mistake and attempts to speak more directly to her audience. She uses the second person pronoun *you* and writes in an altogether more inviting way, though it's a pity she is slightly dismissive when she says *it makes no difference to us*. Instead of facts and figures, she writes about being *transported back in time* and quotes from a boy's contemporary account of working in the mine. Her selection of material is thus much more appealing and the direct address to the readers will be much more successful. She is no longer the austere and distant textbook writer, but someone who is involved both with her readers and with the mine and wants to share her enthusiasm for the subject with her audience. If only she had begun in this way.

Glossing, paraphrasing, simplifying

Read this passage about the possible causes of Multiple Sclerosis (MS).

TEXT 50

Environmental The incidence of MS is higher in countries with temperate climes eg Europe, North America. Possibly diet, lifestyle, physical environment has some causative effect. No theory yet proven.

Genetics Not one identifiable genetic abnormality and therefore not hereditary. Possibly a particular genetic make up causing a susceptibility to develop MS. The familial tendency is presently seen as a child with one parent who has MS being 1% more at risk of developing MS.

Virology No virus has yet been identified as a causative factor. Theories consider the possibility of a dormant virus stimulated by a common virus, triggering the immune response, or an abnormal immune reaction to a common virus.

Immunology MS is now recognised as an abnormal auto immune response. The immune system produces antibodies to destroy the healthy cells of the myelin sheath.

Did you find it easy to understand? Though the author wrote this with an audience of professionals and medical students in mind, you probably would have understood most of what he was saying, because (a) the passage was clearly structured in four labelled parts and (b) the meaning of some of the terms you might not have encountered before such as *virology* and *immunology* could have been correctly guessed from the contextual clues. Only two terms, *myelin sheath* and *antibodies* would be impossible to comprehend without specialist knowledge. However, it would not have been an easy read for you. Why not? Probably the high number of formal terms, most of which are Latinate in origin. Here are two of them: *temperate climes* and *causative effect.*

List the others. Now, imagine that you wanted to use this passage as part of an assignment for relatives, friends and acquaintances of MS sufferers. You certainly couldn't use it as it stands. It would be too difficult, too formal and thus off-putting. You'd need to gloss, paraphrase and simplify. These are three crucial skills you need to develop:

■ to gloss: to give an explanation of an unusual word
■ to paraphrase: to express something in words other than those originally used that still capture the full force of the original
■ to simplify: to make less difficult.

These skills are particularly important to develop if you are writing for a young audience. So in place of the two examples listed earlier, you might want to substitute *countries that don't have extreme variations in their weather* for *temperate climes;* and *some causes* for *causative effect.*

ACTIVITY 30

Identify and rewrite the other terms in Text 50 that might cause difficulties for a non-specialist adult audience.

You saw earlier in the book an example of a writer who included material that she should have glossed. Remind yourself of the passage on Rodin on p 49. Notice how much of the information that she included would have been incomprehensible to her listeners. Her failure to gloss meant that the passage would fail to communicate.

If you use language that is beyond the comprehension level of your audience; if you include information that needs an explanation and you don't provide one; and if what you include is simply too difficult for your readers or listeners, then you too will have failed to communicate. This is, in the context of A-Level English Language, the unforgivable sin.

You can't, of course, gloss, paraphrase or simplify without you yourself understanding what it is you need to gloss, paraphrase or simplify. In other words, if you are taking an exam that allows you time to read the material beforehand, you must ensure, as has already been emphasised, that you prepare it thoroughly and look up anything you don't understand. If you go into the exam not understanding what you are to communicate to others, then you're certain to fail.

ACTIVITY 31

Here is a second extract from the MS document, this time on the treatment and care of sufferers. Re-write it as part of a talk you are giving to a group of fund-raisers for the MS Society, *none of whom are medical professionals.*

TEXT 51

Treatment of a relapse may involve steroid therapy to reduce the inflammation and promote a remission, eg methyl prednisolone usually given IV.

Full nursing care according to daily activities of daily living and altered/changing needs.

Physiotherapy for support during acute period as an on-going therapy. Speech therapy for communication difficulties and for swallowing problems. Full assessment with an occupational therapist and reassessment at times of changing needs.

Information, counselling – it is important that accurate, positive information is available when the individual and their family/carer are ready for it. An honest and positive attitude is essential to help the whole family come to terms with the diagnosis and cope with the uncertainty of living with MS.

Writing for the ear

The previous activity required you to write a text for a talk. Did you read it aloud either during the process of composition or when you had completed the task? If you did, you should have got a good idea as to whether your text would have been successful or whether it needed some further work before it could be delivered. If you didn't test it by reading it aloud, then you might never know whether it was 'speakable'. The writing of texts to be spoken is a very skilful art. Two speech-writers for John Major, a former Conservative Prime Minister, tell of sitting up all night before his speech to the Tory faithful at a party conference, drafting and re-drafting, polishing and honing it and paying close attention to *every* word before the speech was deemed suitable for delivery at the conference and for TV news.

Now it is not suggested that you have the time to do this when you are required to write a spoken text, but you do need to pay close attention to what you are writing and to 'hear' what it sounds like. There is a very close connection between the writer's voice and the reader's inner ear. This, as you have already seen, is true for texts that are meant for silent reading and, of course, is true for texts that are meant for listening to. In a very real sense, you should be writing as both a reader and a listener. In other words, you should be 'hearing' the text as you write and altering it if it doesn't sound 'right'.

Many of the text types that you are asked to write in A-Level English Language are for speaking. You have already encountered some in this book. Spoken texts that you could be asked to write include: radio scripts; speeches and talks; monologues delivered by historical characters; oral narratives; cassette tapes and commentaries for tape-slide shows. Even this list does not exhaust the possibilities. So it is clearly important that you find the right voice for writing speech.

There are lots of texts that we encounter every day that seem to be 'speaking' to us. In such texts the writer often uses features of speech to create the illusion that he or she has a personal relationship with us. Advertisements, information leaflets, Readers' Digest letters, newspaper articles and headlines are among such texts. Here's an extract from a typical advertisement that pretends to be speaking to us.

TEXT 52
Your heart will like it as much as your head

Buying a new car usually involves a lengthy debate between the heart and the head.

At heart, everyone knows what they are looking for. Performance, comfort, reliability and style. The trouble is, that just when you think you have found it, the head comes in and says you can't afford it.

But all is not lost.

Take a look at the Persona range from Proton. Compare the Persona with its mainstream competitors and spec. for spec. You'll save, in most cases, well over £1000. Better still, after 18 months without a price increase, we've just realigned Persona prices offering you a further saving of up to £316.

A Persona has all the features your heart desires. It turns heads because it's beautifully built and gives outstanding performance day-in day-out. It raises eyebrows because it offers models which feature power steering, electric windows and door mirrors, central locking and Blaupunkt in-car entertainment.

And it calms the nerves because reliability isn't just a salesman's talking point, it comes in the form of probably the best long term warranty package in the business. The Proton Customer Commitment.

What's more, the price you see is the price you pay to drive away including number plates, delivery and 12 months' road tax. With Proton there are no hidden extras.

1 Discuss this advertisement and analyse the methods the writer has used to create the illusion of speech.
2 Look back at Text 51. What methods did you use when, in Activity 31, you attempted to write the talk?
3 Collect as many texts as you can that use features of speech and bring them into class.

You could use the Proton advert as a start. In groups analyse and list all the ways that the writers have created the illusion of the spoken mode.
4 Write the A4 side of advice on *Writing for Listeners* that will form part of a supported self-study pack for A-Level English Language students.

A reminder of the warning that was first given on page 28: most speech is impromptu and therefore unscriptable. Don't fall into the trap therefore of writing scripts of interviews, phone-ins or impromptu discussions in radio programmes, for example.

New texts for new ears

Look at these two sentences:

1 Emile Berliner arrived in the United States on 11 May 1870, just one of millions of European immigrants seeking a fresh start in the New World.

2 A man called Emile Berliner arrived in the United States on 11 May 1870, just one of millions of European immigrants seeking a fresh start in the New World.

The difference between the sentences is simple and obvious. But what a difference the addition of *a man called* makes. It alters the way we read it and our perceptions of the intended audience. The first version is taken from a book that introduces the general adult reader to the early pioneers of recorded sound, whilst the second was what one student thought would be an appropriate way to introduce Emile Berliner to an audience of ten year olds. Was he right? To many readers the re-written version may seem too patronising or too immature even for ten year olds. The writer should have considered the effect of introducing someone to a reader in such a way and thought about alternatives. Is there any sort of text in which *a man called Emile Berliner* might be specially appropriate?

This is just one example of what are called the interpersonal features of a text. These are concerned with the relationship between the writer and the reader and though they may often pass unnoticed because they seem an unimportant part of the writing, such details can have an enormous effect on how a reader or listener receives a text. As such, they are very important contributors to tone or voice and you should therefore pay them a great deal of attention in your writing. Other interpersonal features include such things as choice of pronoun (do you use second person *you* or third person *he* or *she* or even the formal and distancing *one*?) and choice of adverb. What, for example, is the effect of peppering your texts with adverbials like *of course, clearly, just, hopefully* and *incredibly*? They affect how an audience 'hears' your text. There are many other interpersonal features that can affect the reception of your text, but there is not space to deal with them all here.

Here is a longer extract from the Emile Berliner text followed by a list of possible audiences. Remember that it was originally written for a non-specialist adult readership.

1 Working with a partner, you should each choose one of the new audiences and re-write the passage or part of the passage for that audience.
2 When you have completed your re-writing, give the new text to your partner for him or her to read. S/he should act as a kind of 'inner ear' for the new text, commenting on where you have been particularly successful in establishing an appropriate relationship with the reader and also where any re-writing is necessary.
3 Re-write your text in the light of your partner's comments.

TEXT 53

The man who made the music machine

Emile Berliner arrived in the United States on 11 May 1870, just one of millions of European immigrants seeking a fresh start in the New World. The nineteen-year-old from Hanover had no obvious skills – and very little education. For five years he drifted from town to town, and job to job, working some of the time as a commercial traveller selling haberdashery from Mississippi riverboats. In 1875, he reached New York, still rootless and penniless, and he found work as a handyman in the laboratories of the man who had discovered saccharine, Doctor Constantine Fahlberg. The laboratory fascinated Berliner, and he began to study in his spare time, reading every book he could lay his hands on. A volume called *Synopsis Of Physics And Meteorology* particularly intrigued him and he read the chapters on acoustics and electricity over and over again.

After a year in New York, he moved to Washington, working by day at a dry goods store on Seventh Street and spending his evenings and weekends in pursuit of the new passion of his life: scientific research and experiment. He turned his bedroom, on the third floor of a boarding house, into an improvised workshop, and began to try and devise improvements for the newly invented telephone. Within a year he had

developed a new kind of transmitter which offered clearer sound and increased the machine's range from two and a half to thirty miles. The Bell Telephone Company gave him $75,000 cash and the promise of $5,000 a year for all rights. He invested the money in a big brick-and-stone house on Columbia Heights, two miles north of the White House, and converted an upstairs room into a laboratory, where he turned his attention to Edison's talking machine. He was impressed by it, but was convinced that it could be made even better. He explored the ideas of other scientists and discovered a paper written by one, Charles Cros, in 1877 and lodged with the Academy of Sciences in Paris. Cros' recording process was similar to that suggested by Edouard-Léon Scott de Martinville but Cros suggested recording on a flat glass disc not on a cylinder.

Berliner started to experiment with the idea that Cros had never had the funds to exploit. He built a hand-driven turntable and made a recording on a round glass plate blackened over a candle flame. He found that the sound quality of a groove made with a side-to-side action was far superior to the up-and-down indentations of the cylinder and the groove also held the stylus in place when the disc was re-played. After countless tests on different materials, Berliner perfected a technique of recording on to a zinc disc coated with a film of beeswax and benzine. When the disc was plunged into an acid bath, a groove was etched in the zinc. But – even more important – a reverse matrix could be made from the disc, turning the recorded track into a raised spiral edge. From this master, hundreds of duplicate discs could be pressed. This was what gave the gramophone an unbeatable advantage over the phonograph, with its non-copiable cylinders. In September 1887, Berliner applied for a patent for the invention which would lead to a multi-million-pound international industry and take music into the homes of all people, in every corner of the earth.

a Ten year olds
b Sixth formers
c People seeking a brief encyclopaedia entry
d Mature learners of English as a second language
e Radio 4 listeners
f Readers of a CD catalogue specialising in historic recordings.

You can, of course, choose an audience of your own if none of the above appeal to you. This type of activity is very valuable because it will make you think clearly about tone or voice in your writing and you should make it a regular feature of your preparation for this part of the course.

Across the desk

A final tip that could ensure you always choose the right voice for your writing. Whenever you write, whether at home, in class, or in the examination hall, imagine that across the desk from you is a member of the audience you are writing for. So, if you're writing for seven to eight year olds, imagine there's a seven year old reading every word you write. Or, if you're writing for senior citizens, imagine there's one carefully scrutinising your text as it progresses. But these people shouldn't be your ordinary, polite readers who will make allowances for everything that you write and think it's wonderful. Instead, they should be highly vocal, perhaps even cantankerous critics. Imagine them loudly voicing criticisms of your text such as: *I don't understand that word!; Why've you included that without explaining it clearly to me?; Why are you speaking to me like that? I'm not stupid!; Don't patronise me!*

Pay attention to these people. Alter your text in the light of what they say, because after all, it's these people you're writing for. They know best! In this way, these imaginary critics will help ensure you use exactly the right voice for your audience and thus guarantee success for your writing.

In this chapter you have learnt:

- the importance of writing in an appropriate voice for an audience;
- that an inappropriate one will alienate readers or listeners;
- that there should be an intimate connection between the writer's voice and the reader's inner ear.

6 Do-it-Yourself

In this chapter you will learn how assignments for this part of your A-Level English Language course are designed and written and how important the mark scheme is.

We are now going to turn the tables on you. Up to this point in the book you've been concentrating on two processes: (i) preparing to write your assignment and (ii) constructing and actually writing your new text. Our aims, therefore, have been to develop your skills and potential as a writer focusing on one particular writing situation, namely your A-Level English Language examination.

Examining examiners

In this section of the book, we shall look at everything that is involved in providing you with the task you face in the exam. Don't worry, you are not being asked to become an examiner! We wouldn't wish such a fate on you! However, there are advantages for you in this approach. If you can experience what examiners have to do when they set their questions: the choices they are faced with, the decisions they have to make and if you know what they hope candidates will write in response, then you should be in a much stronger position to answer any question that faces you in your own examination. And, of course, if you can read the variety of responses produced by a question that you set, you'll be able to judge what would most impress the examiners who will mark your own answers. So, you can see that there are considerable benefits for you in having the tables turned and being on the other side of the fence.

What, then, is involved in designing your own examination question for this part of your syllabus? There are a number of separate stages and we shall be considering each one. They are:

- Choosing a topic for the assignment
- Collecting the material for the assignment file
- Editing the material
- Writing the question or task
- Writing a mark scheme.

These might not always be separate stages, because they can blend into each other. For instance, you might come across some material that you think would be suitable and this could at the same time spark off ideas for a question to you. You should also think about the mark scheme as you write the question. However, each of the five stages has an important part to play in the final outcome, so it will be easier for you if we look at them separately.

Choosing a topic

There are two main sources of help available as you try to decide what topic would be suitable for your assignment: the syllabus for the examination that you will be sitting and the past papers that have been set. Together, these two sources will tell you (i) what is allowed by your syllabus and (ii) how these syllabus requirements have been interpreted by examiners. For example, the syllabus for one examination board suggests that your genre studies should include *history, biography, travel writing, prose fiction, poetry, technical reports, scientific accounts, business and administrative writing (eg, legal contracts, proposal forms, minutes, company records), private and public correspondence, modern approaches to documentary (eg, 'faction'), ephemera (eg, programmes, catalogues, brochures), drama, advertising copy, government publications, news reports, features and editorials, instructional texts.* It also goes on to say that *the range of forms with which candidates should be familiar includes: magazine articles, short booklets for specific audiences and purposes, draft radio scripts (or script writing for pre-recorded tapes) lecture presentations, discussion documents and reports.*

You'll have noticed that both extracts from this syllabus say *should include*; this use of the modal verb means that other genres and other forms are not excluded. Quite daunting, isn't it? On the other hand it does give you a wide range of choices in your new role.

Collecting the material

Clearly, choosing a topic and collecting the material are inextricably linked: it's difficult to know which comes first. Either you start with a great idea for a topic and so have to set about finding material for it or you read something that you think will develop into a good topic and have to set about finding further material. Of course, it's much better, because it's much more enjoyable to work on a topic and material that interests you though, remember, your enthusiasm for the history of tractors built in Lincolnshire or that great new Indie band you saw the other day may not be shared by all your prospective writers. The second example raises a further problem: it's sensible to choose a topic on which you can find plenty of material. There may not be much for you to find on that great new Indie band!

Having chosen your topic, where can you find your material? These are some of the more obvious sources:

- books that you have at home;
- libraries. If you're not sure whether the school, college or public library has material on your chosen topic, or you're not sure where to find them in the library, don't forget that the librarians are usually pleased to be asked to help;
- leaflets, pamphlets, brochures, magazines, newspapers;
- the Internet;
- CD-ROMs.

Don't neglect the less obvious sources, either. Ask around friends and relatives, for example. You never know whether your grandparents might not have kept some old newspapers or magazines or even have material from *their* parents' or grandparents' generation. It's surprising what you can find once you begin searching. Diaries, letters, certificates, for example, could all prove useful. It's obviously impossible to suggest every potential source of material, but it's important to collect as much as you can from a variety of sources. This will give you greater flexibility when you come to make decisions about what to include and what to exclude. It's better to have too much than too little at this stage.

Editing the material

Let's assume then that you've chosen your topic and that you've amassed a range of material from a variety of sources. Let's also assume that you've managed to collect rather too much and that you need to cut it down, as an important principle is that you ought not to overwhelm your 'victims' with too much to read. If they've got too much material to read before they begin writing their assignment, then they won't be able to assimilate it all or make meaningful selections. So what are the principles on which to base your selection? There are nine of them. You should, if possible:

- have no fewer than four and no more than, say, fifteen pieces;
- ensure the pieces are varied in length;
- choose pieces from a variety of authors;
- choose pieces that reflect a variety of genres and styles;
- choose pieces with differing primary purposes;
- choose pieces written at different times;
- choose pieces written for different audiences;
- have pieces that duplicate information. This should ensure that your writers have to make pertinent selections for their new texts;
- have pieces that are contradictory, disagree or put opposing points of view. Again, this should ensure your writers have to think carefully about why such contradictions or disagreements are there and whether to reflect these in their own selection from texts.

You can see from these nine principles, of course, why the advice we gave you in Chapter 1 is so important. You'll remember we told you to prepare the texts you are dealing with very thoroughly before you put pen to paper in the exam. Now would be a good time to remind yourself of the advice that was given in Chapter 1. You might see it now in a new light in your role as question setter.

ACTIVITY 34

You should now, either individually or as part of a group, collect and edit material for an assignment. This, of course, will form the basis for the next stage in preparing an assignment.

Writing the question

You'll remember that in Chapter 2 we indicated that every question or task for this part of the examination has to include four elements:

- the audience for the new text;
- the purpose of the new text;
- the genre of the new text;
- the length of the new text.

Any question that you write, naturally, should adhere to these principles. Remind yourself, again from Chapter 2, of the variety of text types that are available to you as a question setter. You don't need to restrict yourself to these alone. Indeed, you'll most probably be able to think of many additional and perhaps more appropriate ones than those. There is perhaps only one other factor that you need to take into consideration when setting your questions and this is to ensure that you provide a context for the writing. Look back at some of the assignments you have been set either from this book or in class and you will see that they all provide a context which gives a focus for the candidates' writing. These contexts can vary as much as the text types, but here are three examples to illustrate. You'll see that the candidates are not baldly told *write a booklet* or *a wall display* but are given other information to help them.

1 A major petrol company is producing a series of free illustrated booklets about the architectural heritage of Britain, encouraging families to visit places such as abbeys, cathedrals and country houses.

2 A local amateur theatre group is to run a short season of music-hall shows entitled *Those Were the Days*. They have decided to mount a display in the theatre foyer about music hall, its history and traditions for the audience to read before and after the performance and during the interval.

3 Part of your school or college library has been developed as an adult education centre where people can drop in for advice and guidance on a wide range of topics. In conjunction with other community organisations, the centre has produced a series of educational booklets designed to introduce readers to topics of general interest about which they can later seek specific advice from experts.

Each of these examples gives writers sufficient, but not an overwhelming amount of information to enable them to place their writing into a realistic context. Your questions should do the same.

1 a Working in pairs, choose one set of
       material that has been collected and edited
       as part of Activity 34.
   b Discuss the possible tasks or questions
      that could be based on this material.
      Aim for a varied range.
   c Each person should then write one of the
      questions.
   d Discuss each question in great detail,
      examining it closely to see if:
      i there is anything that could possibly
         confuse a candidate;
      ii there are any ambiguities in the
          wording.
   e In the light of the editorial discussion,
      re-write the question in its final
      version, ready to be presented to the
      candidates.

2 Alternatively, choose material that has
   already been used in an examination and
   write new questions based on it. You should
   follow all the stages indicated in 1.

Writing the mark scheme

This is the part of the process that most candidates very rarely see, yet it is
one of the most crucial. If you have spent a long time selecting and editing
your material, if you have deliberated over the precise wording of a
question, then the last thing you want is for the question itself to be
marked badly. You don't want people who have written an excellent answer
to be awarded low marks and vice versa. The key to ensuring that all
candidates who sat your exam are fairly treated is to write a clear mark
scheme that can be applied in the same way to every candidate by everyone
who is marking. It's the mark scheme for each question that should provide
that guidance.

You already know what the important general criteria for success in this
part of your syllabus are because Chapters 3, 4 and 5 focus on these
criteria. These are the structure, cohesiveness and voice of any new text
produced. As such, these three form the basis for the mark scheme for any
question and they remain the same whatever the task, as you would expect.
What we are going to concentrate on now is a specific scheme for one
particular question. This question will be the one that forms the basis of
your study for the remainder of this and for the next chapter. It was used
in the 1998 NEAB examination. Here's the question.

A national tabloid newspaper is publishing a series of articles for parents entitled
Unusual Places to Visit. Each article in the series will feature places of possible
educational value and will include a sewage farm, a gas works, a coal mine and a
nuclear power station. The article should inform parents about what there is for the
family to discover but the editor does not want writers to ignore any reservations they
may have. The purpose of the article is to enable parents to decide for themselves
whether to go on a family visit.

You have drawn off the Internet and from other sources the material about the
nuclear power station and reprocessing plant at Sellafield on which to base a lively
and interesting 1100 word article. Briefly indicate your layout requirements and any
illustrations that might be used.

Here is a summary of the material that candidates had to read and prepare before writing their answers. It's in the order in which it appeared in the assignment file.

- A full colour leaflet detailing what could be seen at Sellafield Visitors' Centre (*British Nuclear Fuels Ltd (BNFL) publication*);
- Extracts from an in-house magazine about research investment at Sellafield (*BNFL*);
- Extract from in-house newspaper about record number of visitors to Sellafield and a new holiday information booking service (*BNFL*);
- Extracts about gas and water releases from nuclear power stations (*US Nuclear Energy Information Centre*);
- Information leaflet about the transportation of nuclear waste and the test carried out to ensure its safety (*BNFL*);
- Material drawn from the Internet about reprocessing of nuclear fuel and concerns about its safety and potential environmental damage (*from N-BASE, an anti-nuclear watchdog organisation*);
- Extract about radiation at nuclear power plants, potential contamination and protective measures taken to counteract this (*from US based 'The Virtual Nuclear Tourist'*);
- Information about key areas and buildings at nuclear power stations (*The Virtual Nuclear Tourist*);
- Briefing notes on reprocessing nuclear fuel (*BNFL*);
- Extract entitled 'Why Does the Public Refuse to Believe the Waste Problem is Solved?' (*Uranium Institute Information Service*);
- Extract from an Irish Republican newspaper about a court case in which Irish residents brought legal action against BNFL for polluting the environment;
- Material drawn from the Internet about the environmental dangers of transporting spent nuclear fuel (*N-BASE*).

This is the mark scheme to accompany the question. Note the formal style that is used in mark schemes:

1 Candidates should demonstrate in their answer awareness of the fact that they have been asked to write for a *tabloid* newspaper, though their choice of newspaper, and therefore appropriate style, may range from the *Daily Mail* to the *Sun*.

2 Lively and interesting writing should be rewarded; there should, of course, be a degree of control exercised by the candidates over their writing and its effects. The best will probably strike a balance between the 'in-yer-face' and the boringly bland.

3 Candidates should structure the information they present in ways appropriate to the genre (eg, teaser paragraphs, summarising paragraphs, important information presented early in the article, etc).

4 Candidates may choose to employ a range of devices to present some information (eg, charts, diagrams, '10 facts you should know about Sellafield', etc). These should be easy to understand, direct and, if appropriate, clearly captioned.

5 Candidates should use headlines, headings, sub-headings etc appropriate to the genre.

6 Illustrations should be appropriately captioned.

7 Candidates must ensure that any scientific or technical information is presented in such a way that the readers of the newspaper can understand it easily.

8 Candidates may choose either a subjective or objective point-of-view, or both. Each (or any other that is chosen) should be judged on its effectiveness in achieving the aims of the task.

9 Candidates should realise that much of the material in the file comes from biased sources and that their treatment of any material that they use should show awareness of this bias.

10 Candidates should remember that the purpose of the article is 'to enable parents to decide for themselves' and that any answer which presents a one-sided view of Sellafield is not fulfilling the editor's intentions. They do not, however, need to be studiously neutral in their article.

11 Candidates should make use of a wide range of source material.

12 Scripts should reflect that the purpose of the article is to inform readers about a potential 'family day out' and that therefore the needs and interests of children should be borne in mind by the candidate.

There are three important points you should notice:

■ The mark scheme is closely related to the question. It stresses very clearly the genre (*tabloid* newspaper), the audience (parents) and the purpose (to inform readers about a potential day out and to enable parents to decide for themselves whether to visit Sellafield) of the article. You can see from this, of course, how important it is for candidates to pay close attention to the wording of any question. Marks depend on it.

■ The mark scheme does not insist on one particular style of answer. It merely states that 'lively and interesting writing should be rewarded' and that candidates 'may choose a subjective or objective point of view.' So every candidate doesn't have to write the same type of answer.

■ The mark scheme stresses that candidates should write and structure their answers in ways that are appropriate to the newspaper genre.

ACTIVITY 36

1 Working in small groups, each person should write a first draft of a mark scheme to accompany the question the group has designed. Make sure that it relates closely to the question.

2 Discuss the suggested mark schemes and decide which one is the most suitable. You may, of course, decide to use parts from more than one scheme in your final version. Check carefully that what is written is crystal clear and free from any ambiguities!

3 Write the final version.

You have now gone through all the stages of setting your question and are in a position to test it out on willing (or unwilling) victims. If you are in the second year of your course, your teacher may be more than happy to use it as part of the first year's preparation for the exam. He or she, we guarantee, will be extremely happy for you to mark their efforts!

In this chapter you have learnt how to:

■ collect and edit material;
■ write questions and assignments;
■ write mark schemes.

7 It's the Real Thing

In this chapter, we are going to look at the performance of candidates in a recent examination and see how A-Level examiners would respond to what was produced.

So far in this book, we've explored the skills and techniques that are required if you are to produce a successful text in an examination. We've also considered the preparations you need to make before putting pen to paper and hope that, if you follow all the advice you've been given, you'll get a high mark. You've even learned how to become your own question setter and examiner!

Now, we'll turn to what candidates actually wrote in their A-Level examination. We won't look at complete scripts, but instead concentrate on some key aspects. Getting these key aspects right in your own work will enable you to gain your best possible mark. All the examples we're going to study are taken from answers to the *Sellafield* question, which you encountered in the previous chapter. So, before reading on, familiarise yourself, if you haven't already done so, with the question, the summary of the content of the assignment file and the mark scheme. You'll find these on pp 75–76.

The opening

It would seem logical to *begin* our look at key aspects of scripts by considering the opening. After all, this will be the first part of a script that the examiner will read and, in many ways, it can be the most important section of any answer. If you get the opening wrong, it can then be quite difficult for you to retrieve the situation and persuade the examiner that this, after all, *is* a good script, worth rewarding. Of course, if this is the *only* aspect of your answer that shows any merit, then no matter how good it is, it cannot fully compensate for the quality of the remainder. So, you can see that it is vital to get the opening right. You'll remember the advice given earlier (p 44) that it sometimes makes sense to leave the writing of your introduction till last.

Remember, too, that the first question any examiner asks of a script is whether what he or she is reading would be effective in achieving its intended purpose. So, let's imagine the situation.

You open your *Daily Mirror* or *Daily Express*, turn to the travel section and are quite intrigued by a short article entitled *Unusual Places to Visit*. You've been looking for somewhere other than Southsea or Alton Towers to take the kids on a day out and this seems just the job. But, *Sellafield?* A nuclear reprocessing plant? You begin to read. You read on. Or do you? The crucial test of the opening of any piece of writing is whether it makes you want to read on. This is especially important for a newspaper article. After all, you don't *have* to read it and there are lots of other articles in the paper competing for your attention. You can soon turn to another or even stop reading entirely and switch on the television. So the opening has got to grab your attention.

ACTIVITY 37

Read the following text, which is the opening to one answer. Write a brief assessment of its strengths and weaknesses.

TEXT 54

The Sellafield Visitors' Centre is off the A595 West Cumbrian coast road and promises an amazing interactive experience containing all the excitement you can handle.

It's a totally different experience that explores and explains the world of BNFL. Designed to inform and entertain the whole family, Sellafield features interactive experiments, intriguing shows and fascinating displays of technology.

Sellafield was set up in 1972 when used nuclear fuel was transported from European reactors for reprocessing.

What is reprocessing?

Once fuel has been put into a reactor and irradiated it is known as 'spent fuel'. There are two different ways to manage spent fuel. It can either be stored in a dry store or underwater disposal, which is the choice for most spent fuel. Reprocessing involves a simple chemical process of dissolving the spent fuel in nitric acid.

COMMENTARY

This is an ineffective opening. It doesn't invite the reader into the article and most would merely glance at it before moving swiftly on. To begin by giving the reader AA type directions to Sellafield is a very tedious strategy. Little context is provided for the writing and, in fact, we are not told what either Sellafield or BNFL are. Though there might well be *interactive experiments* and *fascinating displays of technology* for the visitor, there is no indication that they are on nuclear power and reprocessing. Parents, the intended readership, would be most unlikely to want to take their children to something unknown. Though readers might well guess from the subsequent reference to *nuclear fuel (being) transported from European reactors for reprocessing* that Sellafield and nuclear fuel are not entirely unconnected, what is not required in a tabloid newspaper is a science essay on *What is Reprocessing?* This is what the article seems quickly to be turning into with sentences such as *There are two different ways to manage spent fuel. It can either be stored in a dry store or underwater disposal, which is the choice for most spent fuel.* The examiner will also notice, and be unimpressed by, such things as the writer's stylistic clumsiness in repeating *spent fuel* in too close a proximity, *stored in a dry store* and by the syntactic error of *stored in a dry store or underwater disposal*. All in all, then, this is not an auspicious way to commence the answer.

ACTIVITY 38

Here are six further examples of the start of candidates' answers to this assignment.

1 In pairs, discuss them and rank them in order of their effectiveness as openings to tabloid newspaper articles.
2 Write a brief commentary on each one.
3 After you have done this, compare your commentaries with the ones that follow the texts.

TEXT 55

Unusual indeed! Who would actually think of visiting a nuclear power station? Well, last year 170,000 people not only considered it, they actually went. Of course, they didn't go inside the plant itself, they went to the Sellafield Visitors' Centre. This is a wonder of modern technology, highly computerised and adding to its list of attractions all the time. If money is a worry, fear not. Admission is free. Funded by British Nuclear Fuels Ltd (BNFL) who own Sellafield, the centre is open for visitors to see what really goes on there every day except Christmas Day.

TEXT 56

Firstly, don't be put off by the reputation, rumours and jokes about Sellafield. In our opinion it provides one of the most enjoyable and educational days out available in Britain.

So, what is there at Sellafield?

In short, a lot. Firstly there is the nuclear plant Sellafield is known for. Now, don't be alarmed by this. There is no danger at all. Nuclear plants are licensed on the basis that there will be no undue hazard or significant effect on the public's health or safety. There is certainly a lot that can be learnt about how nuclear energy is made at Sellafield, but there is another aspect that is even more interesting. The Sellafield plant houses one of only three nuclear reprocessing plants in the world.

TEXT 57

As soon as your child is born your only instinct is to protect him, keep him safe from all dangers that today's mixed up world holds for him. You want to be sure that he's safe and healthy and well-fed before he goes to bed every night. The world is a scary place, there is no doubt about that but whereas we see the danger, a child sees everything as new and exciting – something that could be wonderful and change our lives to make them even better. We can learn a lot from our children. However, I am sure that parents across the country got the same reaction of *Oh, Dad, do we have to . . .?* or *Can't we go to the cinema instead?* when a day out at a nuclear power station was suggested and who can blame them? A nuclear power station doesn't sound very enticing, does it? In fact, compared with all the computers and video games and films and music our children experience every day of their lives, it sounds very dull and boring.

TEXT 58

There is a well-founded sense of irony concerning a 'family trip' out to the site of equipment essentially invented for mass scale annihilation. Although Sellafield's purpose is far from that of nuclear weapons, the general public remains sceptical.

Newspapers, TV news, magazines have been obsessed with accusing nuclear power plants of pollution, radiation and contamination for some time now. Open any paper, listen to any news bulletin over a short period of time and Sellafield and Dounreay reprocessing plants will feature, and never too favourably.

TEXT 59

A nuclear power station may not seem like the ideal visiting place for a family day out but in recent years it's become very popular. Sellafield Visitors' Centre in Cumbria is one of the acknowledged pioneers of industrial tourism drawing a record breaking 170,000 people last year. But why visit a place like Sellafield because I immediately think of the bad sides such as radiation – this is the energy given off by radioactive material when it decays. At a nuclear plant there are radiation protection specialists and they check radiation levels. People who work at nuclear plants have to keep their exposure to radiation as low as possible. They wear protective clothing but these are precautions. Nuclear plants are licensed on the basis that there is no effect on the public's health and safety.

TEXT 60

The summer holidays have arrived. Within a week you'll be asked the usual questions: What can we do? Can we go somewhere? Can Lizzy/Jennifer/Angela/Tom/ Philip/Darren come too?

You've heard it all before, haven't you? Children can no longer be happy with an ice cream and a ball! They want computerised fun, games, rides and experimental toys. Well, at the Visitors' Centre at the Sellafield

Nuclear Reprocessing Plant they can get all of this and more. Also, a visit there will prove highly educational – but don't tell the children!

At Sellafield in Cumbria the activity centre is *designed to inform and entertain the whole family*. This interactive experience promotes thought and imagination as the whole family travels from zone to zone (ten in all) watching sound and light shows, having their knowledge tested, taking part in scientific experiments and getting a glimpse into the future. You can also see something of the work of the plant and the massive safety precautions that are taken to protect the environment and the public.

COMMENTARY

Text 55
Lively, arresting opening. Friendly tone. Would make you want to read on to find out what the attractions of Sellafield are. Informative – tells you what Sellafield is and that admission is free. A successful start.

Text 56
A balance of strengths and weaknesses. Begins in an accessible way, seeking to allay fears. Uses sub-headings. Directly addresses its readers, but by Nuclear plants are licensed on the basis … the tone has changed to a mixture of the formal and rather distant. Needs some rewriting to be wholly successful.

Text 57
A very frustrating opening. Well-intentioned, but misguided. Readers would become very impatient with the preamble about protecting your child, especially if this child were a girl, with all the he's and hims. Does try to be lively with references to computers and video games, but this section is introduced too suddenly. A weak start.

Text 58
Worthy, but very dull. Tries to reassure but all the material about radiation protection specialists and protective clothing likely to have the opposite effect. Is informative, but written in a very wooden style – not that of a tabloid newspaper.

Text 59
Very well written. Controlled and organised. Strong sense of a personal voice and point of view. Gives plenty of information in a short space. However, is the tone really that of a tabloid newspaper?

Text 60
Relates to audience and purpose with reference to children and holidays. Addresses readers directly – you've heard it all before, haven't you? Touches of humour – don't tell the children! Doesn't forget to inform about what Sellafield is and what there is to do and see. Lively and enticing. Very successful.

Re-processing

The source material for this assignment contained a great deal of technical and scientific information about the nuclear industry. There was, for instance, information about the re-processing of spent fuel, information about different types of radiation and information about the hazards of transporting nuclear waste over long distances both by land and by sea. The majority of this information would not have been suitable for inclusion in the article without its being rewritten or adapted for its new audience. You can't really imagine having to plough through the following over your cornflakes or whilst on the bus to work, can you?

Radiation levels are normally (in the US) measured in Roentgens/hour (R/hr). The Roentgen is a unit of radiation exposure. The Rem (**R**oentgen **E**quivalent **M**an) is the unit of Dose (actually absorbed taking biological effects into account). The Rad (Roentgen Absorbed Dose) is simply the actual amount of radiation absorbed. The two are related by the relationship:

$$\text{Rem} = \text{Rads x Quality Factor (QF)}$$

where the Quality Factor depends on the type of radiation. Heavy particles such as alphas have a QF of 20, neutrons have a QF of 3–10 depending on the energy of the neutrons. Betas and gammas have a QF of 1.

So, one of the key indicators of success in this assignment was whether the writer managed to make such potentially daunting material accessible to a tabloid newspaper readership. This means that writers had to demonstrate to the examiner their skills of selection, glossing, simplifying and paraphrasing. As you know, these are skills that are central to this component of the examination, no matter which syllabus you are following and they've formed an important part of this book. In a very real way, the writer is re-processing text and it's for this reason that we're going to look at what candidates achieved when they wrote about the re-processing of spent nuclear fuel. Not all candidates, however, included accounts of re-processing in their texts but, of course, they didn't have to. This should serve to remind you that there is no one 'right' answer to assignments; it's perfectly possible for two candidates to gain the same high mark having written two very different answers. If candidates chose not to write about re-processing, yet nevertheless produced a very effective newspaper article, they would still have been rewarded. Let's look at what one candidate wrote.

TEXT 61

I've heard of nuclear power plants, but what's a re-processing plant?

When fuel has been 'used' at a power station it has been put in a reactor and 'irradiated' all the energy that can be usefully and efficiently used. It is then known as 'spent fuel'.

Spent fuel has to be taken out of a reactor when only 3% of its uranium or plutonium (nuclear fuel) has been used. It is for this reason people tend to think re-processing is a good idea.

Yes, but what is re-processing?

Good question! Basically it's a fairly simple process. The spent fuel is dropped in nitric acid which dissolves it. From this solution, experts can separate out the unusable waste from unused uranium and plutonium that can be used again. It's a kind of recycling.

COMMENTARY

This is a script that displays a mixture of strengths and weaknesses. The writer has clearly tried to simplify what is a complex process and has not tried to go into too detailed an explanation. He tells us that *the spent fuel is dropped in nitric acid which dissolves it* and then wisely refers only to *experts* who *can separate out the unusable waste from unused uranium and plutonium.* The style here is slightly clumsy, with too many variations on *used.* He concludes with a positive reference to *recycling.* This second section of the extract is the strongest part. In the first section, though there is a similar desire to be reader-friendly – *it is for this reason people tend to think that re-processing is a good idea,* for example, and to gloss *spent fuel* clearly, he has not proof read his first sentence. It is confusing and needs rewriting. A possible version would be: *For fuel to be 'used' at a nuclear power station, it must be put into a reactor and 'irradiated'. This produces energy. When all the fuel that can be efficiently used to produce this energy is exhausted, it is then known as 'spent fuel'.* The writer has also employed a *question and answer* technique which is quite effective, but which could become irritating if used excessively. With more care, then, this could have been a good opening section. As it stands, it is only partially successful.

ACTIVITY 39

Here are five further examples of candidates' attempts to explain re-processing to the readers of the newspaper.

1 in pairs, rank them in order of effectiveness;
2 write a brief commentary on each;
3 compare what you have written with our notes.

TEXT 62

An aspect which causes concern with environmentalists is something called 'Re-processing'. When fuel has been put into a reactor and irradiated it's known as 'spent fuel' and the nuclear industry manages it in two different ways. The first way is long term storage where the spent fuel is either put in a dry store or underwater. The second way is reprocessing which is a chemical process of dissolving spent fuel in nitric acid and separating out unused uranium and plutonium from the unusable waste.

TEXT 63

Nuclear power stations use uranium ore as fuel which is concentrated in a process known as 'enrichment'. It is then made into fuel rods which generate electricity. They have an average life of four years.

Waste products build up on the rods making them less efficient so the process of re-processing is used to separate the 3% of waste products. Uranium and plutonium make up the other 97% which can be used again. Re-processing means that not as much new uranium has to be mined. For example 15,000 tonnes of uranium has already been recycled.

TEXT 64

Few of you, I assume, will have an A-Level in Physics to understand the technical aspects of the plant. I will attempt to explain and simplify.

Firstly we have the mining of uranium ore which is concentrated by a process called 'enrichment'. This concentrated uranium is then turned into fuel rods which are used to generate electricity. After a period of approximately four years waste products collect around these rods and render them useless – up until they are re-processed. This is when things can get a little confusing.

There follows a chemical process, where nitric acid is used to separate the unused uranium and plutonium from the waste. The unused elements of the mixture then return to be 'enriched' again and used to produce further nuclear power. Simple, huh?

TEXT 65

'Re-processing' is what happens here at Sellafield. There is a highly developed chemical process that is followed to maintain safety standards.

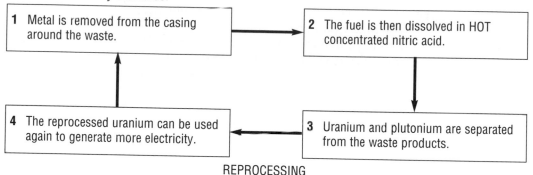

1 Metal is removed from the casing around the waste.

2 The fuel is then dissolved in HOT concentrated nitric acid.

4 The reprocessed uranium can be used again to generate more electricity.

3 Uranium and plutonium are separated from the waste products.

REPROCESSING

TEXT 66

The controversy which surrounds Sellafield is not completely without merit. Sellafield has a reprocessing plant. Re-processing has always been considered in the public and scientific communities as very dangerous. When fuel has been used in a reactor it is 'irradiated' and irradiated fuel must be removed from the core when only 3% of its uranium or plutonium has been used. This 3% is also responsible for 97% of the irradiated fuel's radioactivity. This is when reprocessing is used. By a simple chemical process the usable uranium and plutonium is separated from the unusable waste.

COMMENTARY

Text 62

Simplifies material quite well. Clearly signals methods used *the first way/the second way*. Tone could possibly irritate by appearing to speak down to the reader: *something called reprocessing*.

Text 63

Doesn't include too much information so is unlikely to put readers off by overwhelming them. However, style needs attention: too much *process/reprocessing* and *uranium*. Last three sentences are very wooden.

Text 64

Very aware of readers, directly addresses them in informal way. Process clearly explained in uncomplicated way, with the stages signalled cohesively: *firstly, then, after a period of approximately four years, there follows, then*. A successful re-writing.

Text 65

Good communication strategy to use chart/flow diagram. Perhaps over-simplifies? Not entirely clear what Stage 1 means.

Text 66

No problems with the content of this extract – easy to follow. Style, however, is clumsy, particularly at the start. It is dull and has no sense of being written for a tabloid paper.

The voice

You've seen in Chapter 5 that finding the right voice is essential for success in this part of the examination. However good the content of what you write might be, if it's expressed in the wrong voice then readers or listeners will be so disconcerted or irritated that they will be unable to 'hear' the content and most of the writer's effort will have been wasted. For example, regular listeners to Radio 3 would not be pleased to hear their symphony introduced in the style of a shock-jock from Virgin Radio nor would readers of the *Financial Times* want accounts of company take-overs or changes in share prices to be reported in the style of *Loaded* or *FHM*. So, in this assignment on Sellafield, the best candidates managed not only to include an appropriate selection of material but also to write in the style of a tabloid newspaper. From some of the extracts we've already considered, it's clear to see that many candidates found this quite difficult to do. Some managed the style for a time, but were unable to sustain it and reverted to dull and, sometimes, clumsy writing. You'll have noticed too how the mark scheme draws attention to the requirement to write in tabloid style.

To give you the sound of the genuine tabloid 'voice', if you aren't already familiar with it, here's the opening of a recent feature on an unusual place to visit – a dude ranch in Texas.

TEXT 67

Jason could hit a jackrabbit at 10 feet with a shot of his baccy juice. His *dip* tin, the mark of a real cowboy, made a permanent bulge in the back of his Wranglers.

Do y'all know how to make the horses stop and go? he drawled as we rode out on the trail from the Bar H Dude Ranch.

I grunted nonchalantly, South London's answer to the Lone Ranger. Minutes later I was unmasked. The trail boss bawled me out for overtaking the lead horse at a fast trot.

You have to hold the horse back or he'll tire early, Jason explained. The American Quarterhorse is bred for slow cattle drives from Texas to Montana. But race him and he'll tire after a quarter mile – which is how he got the name.

COMMENTARY Some of the features which give a distinctive 'voice' to the passage are:

- a first person narrator, writing of her personal experience and not afraid to poke fun at herself;
- use of direct quotations;
- informal language intended to give a sense of the American West (*jackrabbit, baccy, dip, Wranglers*);
- short paragraphs;
- vivid word pictures, especially in the first paragraph;
- many dynamic verbs (*hit, made, drawled, grunted, bawled*);
- many proper nouns (*Jason, Wranglers, Bar H Dude Ranch, South London, Lone Ranger, American Quarterhorse, Texas, Montana*).

Let's look at one candidate's attempt to write in a tabloid voice. This example, as are all of these in this section, is taken from the part of the script that deals with the Sellafield Visitors' Centre.

TEXT 68

Report by Ted Bunby, with a little help from his 12-year old nephew, Stephen.

When I first heard that I was given the task of visiting Sellafield, I must admit that I considered 'ringing in sick'. But after considering it for a while, I thought it might not be that bad. My nephew, Stephen was very willing to join me and asked no questions. Indeed, he was really quite excited about the visit.

On arrival at the Visitor Centre we were told that there were two levels of zones to see. The first was the 'Earthzone' which was an intriguing globe that provoked thoughts about the environment and other issues that can affect us all.

We carried on through many different areas of scientific experiments, intriguing shows and fascinating displays of technology which really attracted Stephen's attention. Another good thing that we found about the Centre was that both Stephen and I could touch everything and set experiments off at the touch of a button.

COMMENTARY

This is a script which captures some of the feel of a newspaper article. By being written in the first person, there is a strong sense of a real individual behind it. For example, the writer considered *ringing in sick* when first given the Sellafield assignment. It was also a sensible decision to 'invent' a 12-year old nephew to provide the family perspective that was required. The focus throughout the extract was on what would attract *Stephen's attention* and the reader is thus given a glimpse of what is on offer at the Centre: *scientific experiments, intriguing shows and fascinating displays of technology*. These would be developed later in the article. Admittedly it is not as lively as the article on the Bar H Dude Ranch, but the nature of the two subject matters may have something to do with this. However, the candidate has shown enough evidence that he is aware of the conventions of the genre (including the strap line *Report by Ted Bunby*) and his adopting an appropriate and clear voice means that this can be considered a very successful script.

ACTIVITY 40

Here are six further examples of candidates' writing about the Sellafield Visitors' Centre itself. As usual, we would like you to rank them in order of their effectiveness. The criterion, remember, is how close each one comes to replicating the voice you associate with a tabloid newspaper. Remember, too, that *tabloid* can cover papers from as wide a spectrum as *Daily Star* to *Daily Mail*.

TEXT 69

Sellafield is where it's at! They are racing towards the future at breakneck speed with all the new technology they are at present introducing. British Nuclear Fuels Ltd (BNFL) have just invested a monster sum of £100 million in a brand new technology centre up at Sellafield. The place is jam packed full of computers and interactive experiments that are child's play to operate, but if you should run into any difficulties I'm sure a five year old would be willing to help you out!

Sellafield has plenty of educational value for your family, despite any fears you might have. Nuclear power is the energy resource of tomorrow, so why should we hide it from our children? Sellafield broke all its previous records last year and boasted nearly 200,000 visitors. Can 200,000 people really be that wrong?

TEXT 70

I am going to use these pages to show you exactly what is on offer at Sellafield both for education and enjoyment, but I shall point out both the good and bad points for a day out and leave it up to you to decide if this place is for you and your family.

Sellafield Visitors' Centre which drew a record breaking 170,000 people last year has equipped itself with what could prove to be yet another crowd-pulling magnet . . . one that provides a rare insight into a key Sellafield plant without even going through the doors.

It's called a near Virtual Reality machine, providing a comfortable seat and, hey presto, after a wiggle of the mouse you are transported into the world of Thorp and its amazing technology – a guided tour via wide screen!

TEXT 71

When you first arrive at Sellafield Visitors' Centre you will be given a leaflet explaining what is available for you to do and see, and the option to go on a Sightseer coach on a tour of the Sellafield site. The Visitors' Centre is designed to inform and entertain the whole family. It features 'hands-on' interactive scientific experiments (which are great for the kids), intriguing shows and fascinating displays of technology.

British Nuclear Fuels Ltd (BNFL) has just announced plans to invest £100 million in new research and development facilities at Sellafield. This will help to take the company right into the 21st century.

The Visitor Centre is keen to put over to you the safety measures that they have to ensure that there is only a limited and acceptable effect on the environment. Re-processing is the method by which nuclear fuel can be re-cycled, and therefore re-used. If you visit Sellafield you will discover how used nuclear fuel is transported to the nuclear power station in 'transport flasks'.

TEXT 72

The Visitors' Centre at Sellafield is designed almost purposefully for children with its 'hands-on' activities and zones to take you into the 21st century, not dissimilar to *The Crystal Maze*. Even parents may lose some of their scepticism when given the opportunity to experience the sensation of being in the heart of a nuclear reactor or changing the course of a tornado. There is, after all, a lot to be said for having the power of God in your hands!

With names such as *The Earth House, The Interatom, The Reactor* and *Atomopolis* you can be forgiven for mistaking Sellafield for an obscure nuclear themepark – the Disneyland of Atomic Power.

TEXT 73

The tour will guide you through the site, through all of the buildings which are quite remarkable. The Containment or Drywell Building is a building designed to sustain pressures of about 50 pounds per square inch! It normally houses the reactor and the related cooling system that contains radioactive fluids. It is constructed of steel and sometimes is surrounded by a concrete structure designed for much lower pressures.

The Auxiliary or Reactor Building houses all the support equipment that may contain radioactive liquids or gasses. Emergency equipment is also kept here.

The Turbine Building houses the turbine, the generator, the condenser, the condensate and the feed water systems.

The Screen House houses the circulating water pumps to pump water from the river, lake or sea for cooling the condenser.

TEXT 74

Sellafield Visitors' Centre contains more than enough excitement to take you through to the 21st century.

It explores and explains the truly fascinating world of BNFL (British Nuclear Fuels Ltd). It is a truly entertaining day out for the family to enjoy.

There are a total of ten zones to investigate with actual fun interactive scientific experiments. These include: *The Earth House, The World of BNFL, The Elementary, The Observatory, The Reactor, The Fuel Line, Atomopolis, The Reprocessor* and *The Recyclorama*.

COMMENTARY

Text 69
Attempts a lively colloquial style – *Sellafield is where it's at; jam packed full of computers; Can 200,000 people really be wrong?* And a touch of humour – *I'm sure you have a five year old . . . willing to help you out.* Gives an indication of what there is to see and do at the Centre. Would not be out of place in a tabloid.

Text 70
Begins very ponderously. Wastes time by telling readers what he intends to do, rather than just doing it. Would have lost many readers by this time.

Improves when writing about the Visitors' Centre, but leaves *Thorp* unglossed. What is it? Very little re-writing of source material in final two paragraphs. Too many weaknesses to be wholly successful.

Text 71

Little sense of real engagement with the task. No excitement generated in first paragraph about what can be seen and done at Sellafield. Introduces notions of reprocessing and transportation at this stage. Major weaknesses are dull style that would be out of place in a newspaper and poor transitions.

Text 72

Very informative about what can be seen and done at the Centre. Lively style with references to *The Crystal Maze* and *The Disneyland of Atomic Power*. Shows awareness of the family context for the article – *even parents may lose some of their scepticism*. Wry touches of ironic humour – *There is, after all, a lot to be said for having the power of God in your hands*. A good attempt – more suited to the upper end of tabloid market?

Text 73

A dull trail through four different buildings found at nuclear plants. Doesn't bother to explain technical terms – *condenser, condensate,* and *the feedwater systems*. As it stands, would have few readers. Main problem, however, is that visitors wouldn't see these buildings at Sellafield!

Text 74

Dull, despite attempts to be otherwise. First paragraph is probably the best, but is a direct lift from the Sellafield publicity brochure. Paragraph 2 is clumsy with repetition of *truly fascinating* and *truly entertaining*. Paragraph 3 is a dull list of the names of the zones to be visited, but won't mean much to readers. No editor would give this space in the paper.

Making the links

If you turn back to our comments on Text 71 above, you will notice that one of its suggested weaknesses was that it had 'poor transitions'. Remind yourself of the text itself and you should be able to see what we mean. For instance, there is no link between the end of the first paragraph and the beginning of the second. From writing about the *fascinating displays of technology* that can be seen at the Visitors' Centre, the writer moves immediately to BNFL's £100 million investment in research and development. The two are not related. One is about what can be seen at the Visitors' Centre, the other about BNFL's future unconnected with the Centre. The reader would be left wondering just what the connection is, or if there is one at all, because the writer does not signal any.

Similarly, the third paragraph reverts, without any signal or announcement, to the subject of the Visitors' Centre. This, however, is only for the first sentence. The second sentence changes topic again, this time to a bald definition of re-processing and the third has yet another unsignalled change of topic to nuclear transport flasks. This is very disconcerting for a reader.

So, in a few lines there have been four unsignalled changes of topic. This is what is meant by 'poor transitions' and they should be avoided at all costs.

This was an example of a writer who was unable to make effective and smooth transitions between paragraphs and sentences. We'll now look at two examples of writers who were able to do so. Both are writing about the legal action brought by four Irish citizens against BNFL, in which they accuse the company of making the Irish Sea the most radioactive in the world because of the discharges from Sellafield. The highlighted parts of the two extracts are where the writers do signal their transitions and so make life easier for the readers.

TEXT 75

As you can see Sellafield promotes its work in a very positive way, despite the negative media influences surrounding the re-processing plant. **For example**, four Irish citizens brought an action against BNFL in which they accused them of breaching safety standards and damaging the cleanliness of the Irish Sea and harming the health of local residents. **This** resulted in BNFL issuing new safety guidelines.

TEXT 76

And **finally**, yes, I did have a quite an enjoyable day there myself playing on all the games and acting 12 years old again. But, **don't be fooled!**

Ms Constance Short, Ms Mary Kavanagh, Mr Mark Deary and Mr Ollan Herr **weren't fooled**, and in 1996 decided to fight for their **rights**. The **right** to clean water, safety, health and finally, air they can breathe. **There have been many cases fought** against Sellafield and sites like Sellafield. **There have been many cases fought**, many cases lost and few won.

Ms Short, Ms Kavanagh, Mr Deary and Mr Herr won part of their fight, but the fight for the closure of nuclear power plants all over the world is yet to be fought and won.

COMMENTARY We'll briefly look at the effect of the highlighted pieces of text to see how the writers have signalled their transitions and thus made their readers' journeys that much smoother. We're not suggesting, of course, that these are the *only* ways this can be achieved.

Text 75
As you can see: this refers back to the content of the previous section of the text and thus provides a link between that and what is to follow. *For example*: this demonstrates the purpose of the subsequent reference to the Irish citizens' action. It is included to illustrate the *negative media influences* surrounding Sellafield. *This*: refers back to the legal action already mentioned.

All of these brief illustrations contribute to the cohesiveness of the text and make it much easier to follow. They are the signposts guiding us through and linking the text together.

Text 76
Finally: signals that this is the last part of a section and that therefore

readers can shortly prepare themselves for a new section. *Don't be fooled/weren't fooled*: the near repetition provides a link or hook between one sentence and the next. *Rights/right* performs the same function as does the rhetorical repetition of *there have been many cases fought*.

It is important to stress that there are many methods a writer can employ to provide cohesion and that the ones illustrated may not be suitable for every text. It is, however, important that you try to achieve this smoothness in your own writing; otherwise, your readers will quickly lose interest.

ACTIVITY 41

Rewrite the following three short passages. Each needs this rewriting primarily because of its lack of signposting and poor cohesion. However, you will find that the style of the writing also needs attention.

TEXT 77

If you travel to the world of BNFL you can learn about nuclear safety standards and how Sellafield is developing. When radioactive material decays it gives off energy called radiation. Contamination is when the radioactive material is found somewhere it does not belong. Four types of radiation may be found at a nuclear plant. These are alpha, beta, gamma and neutrons. There has been a lot of publicity about the effects on the public about their health and safety, but the simple fact is that Sellafield could not be safer.

TEXT 78

The Greenland, Iceland, Faroes, Norway and Denmark governments have all protested to Sellafield about pollution of the seas.

If you would like to learn more interesting facts about the subject, then please go and visit Sellafield Visitors' Centre. It is an entertaining day and a truly educational visit.

TEXT 79

There are many activities at the Centre that are said to be both educational and fun. All the activities relate to a different function of the Sellafield plant, not only is the experience fun, but you might learn something too.

Sellafield is basically as safe as houses, the Visitors' Centre is a fun and interesting place, be you young or old so if you find yourself in the area why not pop in and see what all the fuss is about?

Bangs and whimpers

T. S. Eliot in his poem *The Hollow Men* suggested that 'the way the world ends' is 'not with a bang but a whimper'. However, in the rather more mundane circumstances of the A-Level English Language papers that we have been looking at in this chapter, it is much better to end with a bang than a whimper. In other words, you should aim to provide the reader or listener with as strong an ending as possible. We've already stressed the importance of having a forceful and arresting opening; the same is true of your ending or conclusion. This should give your readers or listeners not only a sense that this *is* the end but also a sense of exhilaration, rather than a sense of relief that there is no more that they must plough through. Perhaps the worst type of ending for an exam answer is to leave readers wondering whether what has been written really *is* the end or whether it was the clock that had beaten the candidate. The shape and structure of your answer must be maintained until the final full stop. Nor should you succumb to the tired ploy beloved of dull essay writers of merely repeating in your final paragraph what you have earlier said at length. If you haven't got your message or ideas across by this point, then nothing other than feelings of resentment and boredom in your readers is going to be achieved. Your aim should be to leave them feeling that this was a piece of writing that arrived at a positive and upbeat conclusion and that they would be happy to read more by the same writer. Bangs, not whimpers!

So, let's examine the endings produced by candidates writing about Sellafield. As usual, we'll comment in some detail on the first and then leave you to arrive at judgements on the remainder.

TEXT 80

If you would like to learn more interesting facts about this fascinating subject, then please go and visit Sellafield Visitors' Centre. It is an entertaining day and a truly educational visit!

To gain free entry to Sellafield Visitors' Centre please cut out these coupons and exchange them for a family pass on the door (2 adults, 2 children).

COMMENTARY This is certainly a whimper, if ever there was one. The writer seems to have run out of steam (or time) and readers are unlikely to wish to follow up the invitation to *learn more interesting facts.* The flatness and stylistic clumsiness of the writing (*visit Sellafield Visitors' Centre ... a truly educational visit*) suggests that s/he is not fully committed and that routine concluding motions are just being gone through. Merely using words like *interesting, fascinating, entertaining* and *educational* is not enough if both the writing and content are dull. The article itself should have whetted readers' appetites, if that were the writer's intention. In fact, nowhere in the complete script is there any indication as to the location of Sellafield, so even if readers were inclined to visit, they would find it hard to do so without further information. The second paragraph is redundant as entry to the Visitor Centre is free, anyway. This indicates, of course, that the candidate has not paid enough attention to the source material.

ACTIVITY 42

As before, we want you to place the following six endings in order of their effectiveness. This time, however, you will need to write your own examiner's comments on each of the scripts.

TEXT 81

In conclusion, I felt the trip to Sellafield was quite successful. I asked Susan her view of what she felt was good and her opinion on the parts of the tour she felt were not so good.

'I really liked it in the Visitor Centre because I could go on all the machines and stuff. The trip on the coach was a bit boring, but I liked watching the video about the flasks.'

My advice to anyone wishing to go there would be: Don't take anyone under the age of about 11 years old as some of the information was fairly complex and I feel they would find it difficult to understand. (I did!)

Marks out of 10 = 6.

See our next article on unusual places to visit in the Sunday edition. We'll be visiting a sewage farm! I can't wait for that one – I wonder if Susan will be as keen as last time!

TEXT 82

The Sellafield Visitor Centre provides an interesting day out for all the family. It features 10 zones to investigate, with 'hands-on' experiments making it entertaining, especially for children. In the leaflet you will be given when you arrive the Centre is described as 'All the excitement you can handle'. Although I think this is a slight exaggeration, Sellafield Visitors' Centre will provide a thought-provoking overview on issues that affect us all. It provides an interesting and educational day out for all the family.

TEXT 83

WHERE?	Sellafield Visitors' Centre, Cumbria.
HOW MUCH?	Free
WHAT'S THERE?	Tours, shows, computers, hands-on experience and virtual reality systems.
HANDY HINTS	Get there early. Traffic may be busy during the summer months. Plan to arrive at least an hour before closing time.
OPENING HOURS	Everyday (except Christmas Day) 10am – 6pm (April – October) 10am – 4pm (November – March)
FOR FURTHER INFORMATION	Tel. 01946 727027

TEXT 84

The nuclear industry is a somewhat controversial industry with many opposing views and thoughts.

So, do you want to enter the Sellafield Visitors' Centre? It explores and explains the world of BNFL.

There is hands-on interactive scientific experiments and welcome for the whole family.

BNFL – Where Science Never Sleeps! Can you handle it?

(Next week: a coal mine feature)

TEXT 85

NAME	Sellafield
ADMISSION	Free
FUN FOR	The whole family
IN A NUTSHELL	10 zones of the technology of the future
BOREDOM FACTOR	Very little. Hands-on activities for the kids, whilst parents can do the thinking.
RATING	8/10

TEXT 86

I have now hopefully managed to give you most of the facts about nuclear power, Sellafield and the ethics of the two. I have probably also managed to ensure that nobody reading this article will even consider going there. Well, that's not what I intended to do.

The centre is after all aimed at the kiddies and I don't think that there is a child alive (under 40-ish) who wouldn't have a totally fascinating day, in fact, a fun day. All I'm trying to do is give you the facts you need, so Sellafield doesn't brainwash you into thinking they're something they're not. So teach yourself the facts, then teach your children. Ignorance is not bliss, ignorance can mean the difference between life and death in our future.

In this chapter you have learnt how examiners assess candidates' scripts and the importance of:

- effective openings and closings;
- re-writing the original source material to suit the purpose and audience of your text;
- addressing the readers or listeners in an appropriate voice;
- making effective links between sections of text and ensuring its cohesiveness.

If you follow the advice given throughout this book, you ought to have little difficulty in performing very well in this part of your English Language syllabus. Good luck!